Endorsements

"**The TAO of PIZZA** serves up a deliciously unconventional take on personal growth and prosperity. Mark Hiddleson blends humor, humility, and holistic wisdom into a guide that's equal parts spiritual workout and life philosophy, reminding me that peace, prosperity, and possibility aren't abstract ideals, but everyday choices. If you're ready to trade empty self-help slogans for something real, nourishing, and joyfully human, this book is your next essential read."

—Dr. Jeremy Weisz, Cofounder of Rise25
https://rise25.com/

"Mark Hiddleson's **TAO of PIZZA** is a full-bodied and mature guide to living a rich, meaningful, soulful life. As an editor and collector of spiritual self-help books, I would rank this as one of the better contemporary spiritual guides I've read. Mark explains his concepts in relatable language, with a unique approach, infectious humor, and sincere humility. This is a must-read book for anyone interested in personal growth and spiritual exploration."

—Judy P.

"If you're a growth-minded CEO navigating high-stakes decisions, **The TAO of PIZZA** is a valuable tool. Mark Hiddleson blends practical wisdom with a whole-person perspective that challenges conventional leadership thinking. In my work with CEOs, I see how often they get stuck solving the same problems with the same thinking. This book disrupts that pattern. It reminds us that when we lead from wholeness, our businesses—and lives—start to reflect something far more sustainable and meaningful."

—Andrew Green, Vistage Chair
https://www.linkedin.com/in/andrewdgreen1/

"I didn't expect a book with 'pizza' in the title to punch me in the heart, challenge my thinking, and make me laugh out loud—sometimes all in the same chapter. But **The TAO of PIZZA** did just that. Mark Hiddleson has a gift for weaving deep spiritual truths with real-life stories, humor, and accessible practices that stick with you long after you close the book. This isn't just another self-help book—it's an invitation to remember who you are and how you're connected to everything and everyone around you. As his publisher, I knew it was a special project—but it genuinely shifted how I see my own life."

—Michelle Prince, CEO, Performance Publishing
www.PerformancePublishingGroup.com

"**The TAO of PIZZA** is a surprising and deeply rewarding guide to living with purpose, presence, and joy. Mark Hiddleson blends spiritual insight, personal storytelling, and practical tools with warmth and humor. I've known Mark for over 20 years, and this book reflects exactly who he is—authentic, curious, and deeply committed to helping others grow. A refreshing and relatable read for anyone seeking clarity and connection. Deep insights, big laughs, and practical tools—**The TAO of PIZZA** is soul food at its finest."

—Michael Mikitka, Executive Vice President, MHI Knowledge Center & WERC

"This book is playful on the surface, but bite deeper and you'll find profound, practical wisdom for living a whole, meaningful life. Mark bridges the personal and the universal with rare heart and clarity, offering a framework for growth that's as accessible as it is transformative. If you're hungry for insight, humor, and a more soulful way to live, this is your slice. Profound provocative and playful— **The TAO of PIZZA** is good damn time and a potent guide to a fully engaged, all the fixins life. It's a book that will make you think, make you laugh... but most of all inspire that you live your best life, every day. **Starting today.**"

—Shawn Phillips, NY TIMES Bestselling Author Strength for LIFE

"This is an invitation to an extraordinary journey — a chance to reflect, connect, and grow in ways that are both practical and transformative. Whether you're a seeker, a skeptic, or somewhere in between, **The TAO of PIZZA** offers something for you. Allow yourself to experience a **favorite** dish for **first** time. Let the "Spiritual Lens" expand your perspective and reveal the beautifully interconnected nature of existence. It is **Bon appétit for the soul!"**

—John Allen Mollenhauer, Performance Lifestyle® / Regenus Centers

"From its title to the brilliant content inside this book, **The TAO of PIZZA**, is a wildly joyful dive into living life in its fullness. A compilation of stories, philosophy, spiritual exploration and practical tools, Mark reveals a multi-leveled, holistic understanding of what it means to develop what he has named a "Whole Person Paradigm" — in business and in life!

The river runs deep here as Mark draws on a vast pool of Eastern and Western spiritual traditions along with personal growth practices that span from esoteric to down-home practical. His comprehensive model of cultivating different "Lenses" — Spiritual, Emotional, Mental and Action— is just what we need to embrace all of what is possible in this unpredictable life we have been given. And the lenses are just the beginning!

So does that sound kinda heavy?

Not at all. With a wink and a chortle, Mark manages to tackle the vast subject of human potential with his signature brand of high-spirited humor. I mean, who else could come up with treasures like **"A human is not a static meat suit with a supercomputer brain running the show, somehow connected to an airy-fairy soul** ready to ascend to a cloud in heaven when the meter on the meat suit runs out." —and that's just the tip of the iceberg of grin-inducing phrases that pop up like chocolate chips in the very best cookie.

Read this book to open your mind and heart, laugh, ponder and, most of all, grow."

—Vicki Dello Joio, Author and Founder
of The Way of Joy: A Spiritual Fitness Program
https://www.vickidellojoio.com/

THE TAO
OF
PIZZA

How the Simple Practice of BEing
Can Unlock a Life of Deep Peace,
Unshakable Clarity, and True Prosperity

For Business People and Students of Life

MARK HIDDLESON
with Bettyanne Green

Performance Publishing Group
McKinney, TX

Copyright © 2025
Mark Hiddleson

All Worldwide Rights Reserved.

All rights reserved. No part of this publication may be reproduced, stored in a retrieval system or transmitted, in any form or by any means, electronic, mechanical, recorded, photocopied, or otherwise, without the prior written permission of the copyright owner, except by a reviewer who may quote brief passages in a review.

ISBN:
978-1-967451-11-1 (paperback)
978-1-961781-74-0 (hardcover)

Dedication

To the spirit present whenever two or more are gathered in their name

CONTENTS

Foreword 1
Why You Want To Read This Book 5
Why Me? 21
Innerchapter: We Be Trees! (Nature as our guide) 29

PART ONE

Chapter 1: Spiritual Lens—Picture Possibility 33
Seeing the parts. Seeing the whole. Seeing with energy.
Innerchapter: Tetrahiddle-Haddle Holistic Paradigm Model
(Time for Arts & Crafts!) 61
Chapter 2: Emotional Lens—Passion 65
Principles of pursuit
Innerchapter: Your Dash (Whaddaya gonna do wit it?).......... 90
Chapter 3: Mental Lens—Pronunciation 92
Speak your world into existence
Innerchapter: The Zen of Language (Words are tricky
because worldviews are sticky) 116
Chapter 4: Action Lens—Practice 120
Practice makes permanent (not always perfect)
Innerchapter: FDA Approves First Meditation Pill (a
parody) (Principle of pill as piss poor practice) 145

PART TWO

Chapter 5: Economic Lens—Profession **148**
Put the ECO back in Economics
Innerchapter: An Ecology of Values (Sow the seeds of peace and prosperity) 175

Chapter 6: Effort Lens—Patience................................. **177**
Make it part of your DNA
Innerchapter: Mastery of the Creative Force of Chill (Mind-Body CrossFit) 200

Chapter 7: Tuning Lens—Pertinacity **203**
Fine-tune your awakening process
Innerchapter: The Prince and the Sharpest Knife................ 225

PART THREE

Chapter 8: Circular Cyclical Lens—Process **228**
Expand the edges of the container of consciousness
Innerchapter: The Practice of Freedom............................ 249

Chapter 9: Community Lens—Contribution **252**
[Re]Connecting to community with strength, unity, and resilience
Innerchapter: The Natural Evolution of Social, Economic, and Structural Networks (a history).................278

THE END... And an Invitation to Begin 287
Wrappin' It Up: A Poem by Mark Hiddleson 297
Acknowledgments 301
Chapter Notes and Citations... 305
How to Contact Mark Hiddleson 331

FOREWORD

Pizza is universal. It transcends cultures, generations and tastes, much like the wisdom that unfolds in these pages. At first glance, *The Tao of Pizza* might seem whimsical, but peel back the layers, and you'll find a deeply thoughtful exploration of how the simple, circular pie we all love serves as a metaphor for life, connection, and spiritual awakening.

Mark Hiddleson is a modern-day philosopher and practitioner of holistic living who approaches spirituality not as dogma, but as a dynamic, lived experience. Through years of study, teaching, and practical application, he's developed a passion for guiding others in his everyday life as a family man and businessman. He shows us how to live through the Whole-Person Perspective inherent in all of us, offering a new and relatable framework for seeing life with clarity, purpose, and a profound possibility perspective.

WHY THIS BOOK, AND WHY NOW?

We live in an era of paradox. The digital age connects us in ways previously unimaginable, yet leaves many feeling more isolated than ever. We're bombarded with information but often lack wisdom. *The Tao of Pizza* is a much-needed pause—a moment to reimagine what it means to be human in a fast-moving, complex world. It bridges the gaps between the personal and universal, material and spiritual, parts and whole. Through the metaphor of pizza, this book playfully yet profoundly examines how we can cultivate wholeness in our fragmented lives. It takes us from the granular "parts"—our daily actions and thoughts—to the transcendent "whole"—our connection with the spacious, boundless energy of the universe.

A PERSONAL CONNECTION TO THE AUTHOR'S VISION

I've had the privilege of knowing Mark personally and spent a unique year with him in a three-person workshop with Shawn Phillips (*Strength for Life* and *Zen of Strength*). I can attest to his ability to live from a deeply holistic sense of himself while making even the most profound spiritual principles tangible, approachable, and fun. I mean, we're talking about *The Tao of Pizza* here!

Mark's primary business is offering warehouse racking solutions. So, what is he doing writing a book like this? It's because he cares as much about the lives of his clients as he does about delivering the solutions they need for their businesses. He genuinely cares about you, your well-being, and the life you are living. That's exactly why you'll want to keep reading.

His vision for this book didn't come from an ivory tower of abstract thought. It came from a desire to help people live fuller, richer lives—starting right where they are and using tools as simple as humor, mindfulness, and even rosemary sprigs.

WHAT YOU'LL FIND WITHIN THESE PAGES

Readers of *The Tao of Pizza* can expect a delightful blend of storytelling, practical exercises, and deep spiritual insights. Each chapter invites you to see life through fresh eyes, offering a step-by-step expansion of your Spiritual Lens—seeing the parts, seeing the whole, and seeing with energy.

You'll learn how to clear the "dust" off your mental mirror, embrace the interplay of opposites, and savor the process of growth—much like enjoying the perfect bite of pizza. The lessons presented here are universal, transcending any one faith or tradition while remaining grounded in principles that resonate across human experience.

This book offers something rare: a roadmap to wholeness. It invites you to bridge the gap between the external pressures of daily life and the internal yearning for peace and purpose. It's a guide to embracing the interconnectedness of our spiritual, emotional, mental, and physical selves, empowering us to live with clarity and intentionality.

Drawing from Mark's deep exploration of diverse philosophies and practices—spanning Taoist principles, holistic health, and human performance, this book challenges the conventional paradigms that often confine our potential. It's not just about theoretical insights; it's a call to action to rediscover your gifts and recalibrate your approach to energy, relationships, and personal evolution. By weaving together practical wisdom and accessible tools, it becomes a manual for unlocking the profound yet often untapped possibilities within each of us.

YOUR INVITATION

This is more than a book; it's an invitation to an extraordinary journey. It's a chance to reflect, connect, and grow in ways that are both practical and transformative. Whether you're a seeker, a skeptic, or somewhere in between, *The Tao of Pizza* has something for you.

So, as you turn the pages, allow yourself to approach life with the curiosity of someone tasting their favorite dish for the first time. Let your perspective expand and your mind and heart open to reveal the beautifully interconnected nature of existence.

Bon appétit for the soul,
John Allen "JAM" Mollenhauer
Performance Lifestyle® Coach
Founder, Regenus Centers

WHY YOU WANT TO READ THIS BOOK

I wrote *The Tao of Pizza* because the Tao of Physics was too hard (Fritjof Capra already did an awesome job of it in his exploration of the parallels between modern physics and Eastern mysticism).

Let me start over... I wrote *The Tao of Pizza* to connect with and reach **people interested in realizing their highest potential.** Whether it's starting a business, generating a body transformation, crushing it in your career, or seeking to enjoy deeper relationships, most people get stuck at some point. This book was created to unstick stuckness and stickiness to clear your path to live and BE in peace and prosperity.

Do we need another spiritual self-help book or, for that matter, one more book about pizza??

Yes, we do! As long as there is domination of these "five cancerous behaviors" that inhibit a person's ability to grow and thrive:

- Criticism
- Complaining
- Comparing

- Competing
- Contending

These are all sources of suffering and lead to unhealthy or addictive behaviors. They reinforce the cultural dialogue that continually plays the message in our heads that we are not good enough, attractive enough, have achieved enough, or acquired enough material possessions. This social pressure is typically and specifically designed to sell us a product that promises to deliver us from the misery that the message created in the first place!

I believe every human plays a role in creating THEIR OWN reality, in business and life, by first deciding what that is and then organizing their priorities around achieving it. Here's why: The truth of it all is that ***your reality will happen whether you are intentional about it or not.*** And guess which way is preferable and more profitable?

Reality without intention means to submit to the messaging, follow the rules, swim in the mainstream lane, clock in, and, eventually, clock out. Don't think or feel too deeply; don't ask "why."

This is definitely a way to go... but I don't believe that's why you picked up this book. You want to rise above the seductive social messaging that kills. To activate your highest potential for peace and prosperity. To access possibilities beyond your current reality. To make wise decisions and solve problems. To make a difference in the world. And... to have a really good time while you're here on this planet!

As a kid, I was curious about ideas I would now call "spiritual." Ever since I was a teenager, I've been fascinated with evolving in the personal, professional, and spiritual aspects of my life. And—funny thing—the greatest lessons I've learned in life have appeared in the form of the most ridiculous mistakes I've made. Embracing the lemons-to-lemonade philosophy and values has kept me on my path of integration and growth. And I want to share a few of the things I've learned and mastered (and some that I am still fighting against or wondering about).

I think of myself as a serious dilettante, buffoon, world traveler, spiritual seeker, husband, father, entrepreneur and citizen. I've started a few businesses and helped others start theirs, earning an M.A. in Holistic Health Education and taking leadership roles in community causes along the way. The throughline has been researching and learning "holistic thinking" that I can apply to my spirituality, health, relationships, wealth creation, and making a contribution to the community at large.

This deep and motley combination has led me to write *The Tao of Pizza* in the hope that my ideas, studies, and personal journey will help you create the life you dream of—by tapping into YOUR OWN WAY of going about it.

So, you have my express permission to take, love, use, or kick to the curb anything you read herein!

ABOUT THE TITLE

The choice of the words "Tao" and "pizza" is intentional. Words can be tricky, and I'll tell you right now that you're in trouble if you try too hard to make sense of the title, so relax and flow with me here...

At the heart of the *Tao* are the non-rational, non-linear, non-dual aspects of reality that are real but indescribable in words because of the very nature of Tao. And if you say you understand this, you're probably full of shit, and you'll get a lot out of this book. If you're honest and say this doesn't make a shit lick of sense, then you will *really* get a lot out of this book (because that's what my editor says, and she's pretty smart and has been right about almost everything).

Tao, simply put, means "way of nature." Said another way, "we are nature," so it's about us—all people. That might sound a little woo-woo, but it's the most common-sense thing I've ever heard of (and it's backed by science).

What else would we be?

So, the concept of *Tao* is the undividable whole, eternal and ever-present in all things. MUCH more on this later. For most of my adult life, I engaged in Taoist practices without knowing it. My "spiritual fitness" instructors, like Vicki Dello Joio and Wendy Palmer, didn't call it that. They were smarter and better trained than I was.

Pizza, on the other hand, can be sliced up and passed around at a party. It goes really well with beer, too, especially for Monday Night Football. The *Tao* can't be divided into slices, and I don't know if it goes well with beer. No, wait, everything goes good with beer. See? That's how it works … our lives are made up of the whole and eternal AND the slices of moments that happen while we're planted firmly on the earthly ground.

What creates our reality is the force and influence of both the spaciousness of all that is and the specific thoughts and actions we have every day. It's all connected and flows together to make us who we are—and can be.

Maybe that makes sense?

"Pizza" in the title represents the paradigms, principles, and practices (including societal messaging) that make up our lives in the world. We tend to live by these, whether they are helping us or harming us, usually without our awareness (we all know that pizza isn't good for us, but it just tastes too good). Our ability to shift our paradigms, examine our practices, and be honest with ourselves about the systems and processes in our collective society is as delicious as a supreme pizza with the works!

> "The more you lose yourself in something bigger than yourself, the more energy you will have."
>
> —*Norman Vincent Peale*

The ***Tao of Pizza*** is about understanding and using these forces to choose differently in and for our lives. These shifts—if we choose to make them—are the first steps on any journey toward elevating the human experience. And did I mention having a good time while we're at it?

THE SPIRITUAL GYM WORKOUT

I'm not going to plug one "silver bullet" approach (and get a cut of the deal when you buy) because I don't believe there is one.

If you've ever worked out at a gym, you know that your workouts are curated in combination to get the best results for your whole body. If you only did your arms, you'd look like a goofball; you have to do your arms, chest, back, and shoulders. Same with your legs and your core.

When it comes to your spiritual fitness, one person will tout yoga, another mindfulness, another positive thinking or Law of Attraction, organized religion, and on and on. All of these are fine, **but you want to develop the whole person, not just their parts.**

In the same vein, people will tout that affirmations will get you what you want. I'm going to give it to you straight: **Affirmations don't mean anything unless you have done the other work** to identify what you really want, release what's blocking you from getting it, embed the energy of the affirmation you choose and know what actions to take to BE the energy that generates that desired thing.

Here's the punchline: In the same way that understanding anatomy will help you work with your muscles and tendons more effectively, understanding the basics of how you approach, view and navigate the world will help you get to the root of what's stopping you from accomplishing your most audacious goals, enjoying the relationships of daily life and making a difference to create a world that works for everybody.

Welcome to the Spiritual Gym Workout!

THE WHOLE PERSON PARADIGM

"Holistic perspective" means encompassing the whole of a thing, not just the part; seeing and accepting ourselves as a whole—the good, the bad, and the ugly of what it means to be human. When we have a holistic perspective, we can proactively create a lifestyle that supports healing relationships and generates the energy to accomplish the biggest things we want to do in the world.

I have developed a model around this concept, which I use in coaching and in my own business, called the **Whole Person Paradigm**. It's a holistic, fundamental spiritual/personal growth workout that draws from wisdom and practices from the East, West, and pretty much everywhere in between and across the time (and space) continuum.

My intent is to make this information available for you to find better ways to connect with yourself, in relationship with other people, and with *Tao*, the spaciousness beyond all distinction.

The key: **Getting to the ultimate source of our energy, vitality and wholeness starts with freedom from the prison that makes us feel separate from everything else.** We then live, practice, and grow in that awareness and apply holistic thinking and problem-solving to our businesses, family, and community relationships.

Through this book, I want you to be able to create a Whole Person Paradigm for yourself!

The Whole Person Paradigm makes available better ways to connect with happiness in a meaningful way. Happiness isn't having sports cars, nice houses, and all that, though they're great to have, and I still want those things. But when I look back, the things I've acquired and the successes that have brought me happiness have all come through relationships. Somebody taught me something, took me under their wing, invited me to their house, or introduced me to other people they knew. From them, I learned new experiences and shared great times together. THIS is what has brought me true happiness!

Happiness is about how we create our particular reality through our connections with each other. Innovations in the last hundred to a hundred fifty years have yielded some amazing benefits to us humans. At the same time, there are some pathologies to the approach that got us here—centrally, the reductive, scientific, mechanistic, or materialistic paradigm.

Contemporary humans have lost sight of the fact that we are Tao, we are nature, and we are interconnected. We need to shift our perspectives to be more humanistic and holistic, because that's where creativity and innovation (and happiness) really happen! True innovation begins with people. No matter how great your processes, tools and technology are, if you don't have the right people and relationships, you're screwed.

> "The purpose of life is to discover your gifts,
> and the meaning of life is to share them."
>
> —Bill Hiddleson

My dad, Bill Hiddleson, told me this in his late seventies while we were going over his will. I don't know where he heard it, but he meant it, and it describes the Whole Person Paradigm perfectly. The essence of this practice is awareness and the acknowledgment of three opportunities every person is born with:

1. The freedom to **choose**
2. The natural laws and principles that dictate the consequences of behavior. Positive consequences come from **fairness, kindness, respect, honesty, integrity, service, and contribution**
3. The four intelligences—**spiritual, mental, emotional, and action** (more on these in a moment ...)

These incredible opportunities form the foundation of this book and show how you can BE the path to peace and prosperity.

THE TETRAHIDDLE-HADDLE HOLISTIC PARADIGM MODEL

The backstory...

The tetrahedron, a four-faced triangular pyramid, is a practical model for encapsulating my concept of the Whole Person Paradigm. I affectionately call it the Tetrahiddle-Haddle Holistic

Paradigm Model (detect the hint of a high-school nickname in there somewhere?) or THPM.

> "Within [the tetrahedron] lies the energy that holds all life together. The bonds that hold atoms, particles and molecules together, all the way down to nanoparticles and all the way up to macroparticles, are tetrahedral. Everything that exists as you conceive of it in a 3-dimensional world is held together by these tetrahedral bonds."
>
> —*R. Buckminster Fuller*

This compelling quote might give you an idea as to why I jumped at the chance to use a tetrahedron to bring sense to the Whole Person Paradigm concepts for myself and to share with others. Bucky Fuller's fascination with the tetrahedron lies in its inherent structural stability and the interrelationships among its sides and edges, all of which do a good job of representing a 3-D world.

Let me start off by assuring you that this information isn't meant to be memorized or comprehended on a mathematical level. It's meant to give you a visual structure of what we'll be talking about throughout the book (and it reminds us of a pizza slice!). **The THPM is an elegant tool to create the space, literally, to understand concepts that are very real to our lives but without easy-to-discern dimensions.** You'll learn how to use these concepts in your life as we go along.

And don't worry, there's an integrative arts and crafts project coming up that will allow you to understand this idea in ways words in a book never could—to practice new ways of BEing on your path to peace and prosperity!

In the Whole Person Paradigm, each of the four triangles of the tetrahedron represents a facet of human existence:

Spiritual
Emotional
Mental
Action

These aspects are interconnected, much like the interlocking triangles of the tetrahedron, suggesting that our well-being relies on the balance and integration of all four faces. I call them lenses: Spiritual Lens, Emotional Lens, Mental Lens, and Action Lens.

The tetrahedron's triangular faces offer symmetry and equilibrium. This signifies that we generate space and maintain balance across spiritual, emotional, mental, and action dimensions to have better (and better!) problem-solving and well-being. Neglecting any facet could lead to instability, which would hinder holistic growth.

The edges of the tetrahedron represent our six fundamental human gifts:

Self-awareness
Imagination
Sensation of the Six Senses
Inner Voice
Choice
Sense of Humor

In the THPM, each triangle shares a corresponding gift with the edges that connect them. For example, the Spiritual Lens (which we'll start with in Chapter One) has its particular gifts (sides of the triangle), which are self-awareness, sensation of the six senses, and sense of humor. The Emotional and Spiritual Lenses share the "edge" gift of the sensation of the six senses. All four Lenses are interrelated in this way, sharing three fundamental human gifts, expressed through that particular lens.

By seeing these interrelationships, you will be able to identify possible imbalances in these major areas of your life. You'll look at the nuances from a heightened self-awareness and make choices that will fuel your energy on the Whole Person Paradigm path.

HOW TO USE THIS BOOK

This book is like a manual you will want to go back to and draw from again and again. I have used this book with my company's team to explore new and different ways to work and problem-solve together. A LOT of stuff has come up for people, including breakthroughs breaking through!

For your first time, I recommend you start at the beginning because each concept, especially in Part One, builds on the previous one. **Part One** covers the four Lenses through which we see ourselves and experience the world. **Part Two** offers areas of practice, and **Part Three** *really* gets into it, exploring expanded consciousness and living.

Each chapter in the book includes a section called **The Payoff**, which covers ways you can apply the learnings to your business and personal life.

At the end of each chapter is a section called **Going Deeper**, which includes a simple practice to help you integrate the chapter content and a kick-start activity to get you moving forward. These practices only take a few minutes, but they will open up possibilities, ignite passion, and put the action into the law of attraction for your peace and prosperity.

My hope is that you'll be able to connect the dots between the capabilities of your mind, body, and spirit, and find the most natural and authentic way of pursuing your most audacious goals in the areas of life that matter to you most.

You'll probably find a weird combination of airy-fairy and kick-ass. That's where you get to use your incredible "freedom to choose" opportunity to create and engage your own practices and make them as airy-fairy or kick-ass as you like. That choice is up to you, and believe me, the world needs both!

THE INNERCHAPTERS

While I love to get into the weeds of (and talk about with anybody who wants to listen) a broad expanse of philosophy, psychology, sociology, anthropology, ontology, phenomenology, and other "ologies," *I want this work to be accessible, easy to digest, and simple to apply right away.*

So, between each chapter, you'll have the choice to hop into the weeds with me to go more deeply into a topic as explanation, research, story, or poem. And there are even more weeds, reeds and doable deeds to play among in the **Notes and Citations** at the end of the book.

SPIRITUAL DISCLAIMER

I always apologize for my lack of knowledge in these things because I know of the Masters who have studied and embodied the principles of life over the last few thousand years. My understanding may not compare to that of a guru or sage, so I am humbly attempting to follow in their quest to understand the Tao.

My spiritual practice leans more toward Christian-Buddhist-Taoist-Zen (CBTZ). Christian because of the culture I grew up in. Once you've experienced Christian salvation—the humility in asking for it and the subsequent rebirth and liberation—you can't undo that experience. I believe it must be what is meant by nirvana, enlightenment, Zen, or those experiences in life that are so vivid and real, like the day you witnessed your child breathe their first breath and cry their first cry. In an instant, you're transformed—a completely different person in the world.

I dabbled in Taoism and other Eastern philosophies early on, and I believe it is important to honor those traditions as they were before I got my hands on them and put my twisted Christian values, conscious capitalist ethics, and passions onto them! In doing my homework in philosophy, I discovered that the mind-body problem is called the "hard problem." Okay, about twenty-five years ago, my goal in life became to "solve the hard problem." Geez, gimme a break.

I've been to over forty weekend retreats, training in practices from Qigong, Aikido, Shamanism, Reiki, Shamanic Drumming, Somatics, and Chinese Medicine in Spring Diet (I had no idea it was a cooking class until thirty minutes into the four-day retreat). As a result, I've never focused solely on one area but hybridized all of these practices, which creates a sort of practice blender to generate one I can call my own.

I want to mention a few of the masters I've trained with and have adapted some of their practices: Wendy Palmer, Joy (Vicki Dello Joio), Pastor Dave Patterson, Shawn Phillips, and JAM (John Allen Mollenhauer). My hope is, and I hope they will agree, that their practices have been recycled, repurposed, and reused within these pages for good.

The prose and poetry are mainly my own vernacular, and hopefully, my errors of grammar and colloquialism and sometimes colorful language serve to inform and entertain. If you're one of those grammar-hungry, hissing, howling academics who will point to an author's lack of tactical grammatical expertise to refute the gravity and severity of the work, go read *Huckleberry Finn*. (Maybe you can see I'm a little sensitive on this issue?)

The Tao of Pizza is a humble appeal to transformational, rather than informational, learning. We are moving beyond the Information Age because we're overwhelmed by information. Our personal information has been stolen and sold to the highest bidder, and the problems we need to solve often seem impossible from where we stand.

Why not try something else—some new ways of BEing?

The Tao of Pizza is here for you as a resource for this transformational age, to create a Whole Person Paradigm for yourself, one that you can love and live in. And I want you to laugh at how life can be so humbling, yet so extremely enjoyable.

So, dive in, and let's have a good time...

HEY, WHY DON'T WE GET STARTED RIGHT NOW? Here's a kick-ass practice to help you visualize the THPM: Thinking of the six gifts I listed earlier—**Self-awareness, Imagination, Sensation of the Six Senses, Inner Voice, Choice, and Sense of Humor**—choose a color to associate with each gift, and write it down on a 3x5 card, cocktail napkin, journal, or in this book. There's a NOTES page between each chapter for your pleasure or pain. (I used to struggle with defacing a book by writing in it; after years of therapy, I'm having fun with it now.)

You'll find out what to do with it later on...

WHY ME?

You might be picturing me as sinewy and lanky with long, naturally graying hair, living off the earth, wearing Birkenstocks, born into a pious and spiritual life, and traveling with a singing bowl and sage. You couldn't be further from the truth (except for the Birkenstocks)!

I was a big, brash, tough, outdoorsy kid growing up in the rural Central Valley of California—the exciting territory of legendary Chief Stanislaus (born as Cucunichi of the Miwok Tribe), who led a rebellion against the Spanish and Mexicans in 1828. My family lived in a beautiful spot near the river, perfect for an adventurous and freewheeling childhood.

My home life was full of love and, at times, also chaotic, unsettling, and sometimes violent. At a young age, I witnessed some things I shouldn't have. When I was eight years old, my mom left my stepdad, who was a good man and likely suffering from the trauma and readjustment of returning from war. After my mom left him, some caring soul told me, "Well, now YOU'RE the man of the house." I took that to heart, along with a strong sense of protecting the underdog and a responsibility to make sure everyone was okay, especially my mom and little sister.

So, I took on a lot of stuff at a young age and had to grow up too fast—but I don't see any of it as good or bad. It just happened, and helped form the person I am today, most of which I'm pretty happy with.

My one constant has been my mom (I even interviewed her recently on my *Tao of Pizza* podcast). She's my hero, a beautiful person and one of the greatest teachers in the world. My mom has spent a lifetime identifying creative ways to elevate learning, bringing in music, poetry, role-playing, and movement to inspire her children to learn, particularly kids with learning disabilities or ones for whom English is their second language. She brought music into my life. I remember singing with my grandparents, mom, and aunt around the piano over countless holidays. Her creativity, love of learning and reading, generosity, and care for others have influenced me.

The community I was raised in was really small, kind of the California version of the Texas Bible belt. There were more churches than anything else, and I was surrounded by religious people. My mom's parents had been raised with traditional Christian values; my mom and her sister had more liberal ideas about religion, so we weren't churchgoers growing up. I had an interesting mix of influences—devout, traditional, casual, atheistic, and a little San Francisco woo-woo.

I was curious about all of it and interested in the Bible as a historical record. To me, the writers were the smartest people ever in a time when not everyone could read or write. They had some valuable things to say. I began noticing that people in communities of faith felt more engaging to me, had more friends, and were more successful in business. They seemed more peaceful than other people. My Aunt Larry and Uncle Frank were spiritual people, and I can still feel Uncle Frank's warmth and love in his handshake as if it were yesterday.

Basically, I was brash and sensitive, wild and wanting to be a good son to my mom, curious and rebellious, cocky and spiritual. As I grew a little older, I began to question more about religion, calling out a lot of folks who didn't know shit about it (at least in my young mind). Eventually, I decided I would just do MY OWN version of "religion."

BASEBALL AND THE MIND-BODY CONNECTION

My dream in life as a teenager was to be a baseball player. Obsessed over what people with money and happiness could attain, I was young, naive and cocky enough to think that I could have all this as a pro player. My new stepdad guided me through my early years in youth athletics. I trained harder than most of my peers, and by the time I reached high school, I had already played on traveling teams, won championships, and was recognized as a straight-A scholar-athlete and All-League championship pitcher.

As a wide-eyed first-year student in high school, I was buzzed to be attending a baseball coaching clinic at Solano Community College with my stepdad, who was now my high school baseball coach. This event was about coaching for coaches, so I was in awe, sitting among hundreds of amazing adults and listening to the presentations of ten Division I instructors.

I really sat up and paid attention when Bob Milano, head baseball coach at the University of California-Berkeley, got up to speak because it was my dream to go to Cal. He talked about something I had never heard of before—and it would change my life forever.

Bob shared with the group the importance of the mind-body connection, explaining how when you heighten your physical sense, your mind is more susceptible to using positive visualization to enhance your performance. He described exactly how he did it as a coach: At the end of a practice, Bob would lead his team through a grueling conditioning workout—running sprints, pushups, demanding drills, and the whole bit. He would push them hard, then gather them, dragging their feet and gasping for breath, into the outfield. He would then have everyone silently lie down in the grass, close their eyes, and imagine themselves succeeding on the field. They pictured the perfect swing, the precise pitch, and the electrifying moments of victory.

It blew my mind!

I could not wait to try this out myself. The next time I went to practice, I pushed myself as hard as I could, then lay down in the field. I focused on my goals as the fatigue from the conditioning melted away. **I could viscerally feel the connection between my mind and body.** I immersed myself in the mental imagery of success. It was as if my dreams were becoming tangible.

This unique blend of intense physical conditioning and visualization opened up a new world of possibilities for me. I began making it my regular practice and even told my best friend (a catcher) and two of my teammates about it. We started visualizing together.

In our seventeen-year-old hearts, we believed that this practice was how we won the League Championship, and I was voted Best Pitcher by the coaches in our league!

What I know today is that whether or not this practice brought winning results isn't what matters. The power of visualization, especially combined with rigorous physical activity, was shaping my skills and also my destiny. It was a turning point in my personal development journey. My life was transformed in a way that went far beyond achieving things—and it would help carry me through some turbulent high school years.

THE BUTTERFLY EFFECT

When I look back at high school, I see the dark side of the Hiddleson journey. I played baseball, basketball and football. As a freshman, my friends and I thought the guys on the varsity football team were gods, and we mimicked a lot of their behaviors. These guys were mostly idiots—not because they were actually idiots, but because they were seventeen and eighteen years old, on top of their game and on top of the world, immortal and believing that playing by the rules didn't apply to them.

The behaviors we mimicked weren't always healthy.

So, as behavior patterns go, when we got to varsity level we became the BMOC, the jock kings, the gods the younger guys looked up to. What they saw in us was, *Hey, this is how you get to be a great athlete and be cool,* so they mimicked our behaviors, which meant breaking the rules and adopting a proverbial lifestyle of "sex, drugs, and rock and roll."

Years later, my high school friend and I would talk about this (he's now a teacher and football coach). We knew we had set a terrible example for those kids who looked up to us. It hurts to look back on this period. It hurts right now to write about it, especially when I think about a few of them who got involved in drugs or more serious things and never made it out.

We create something that's going to endure, and whether we do it on purpose or not, we are creating. I created my high school personal culture. I created an example for those kids. We're all creating things that endure. And that's the reality of human nature.

It's Edward Lorenz's Butterfly Effect, which describes how small actions or changes can lead to significantly different outcomes.

This high school experience is one reason why I have worked so hard to create something different in myself and for others. It is why I'm passionate about coaching kids and helping at-risk youth. That's why I'm writing this book.

An injury prevented me from going any further than high school baseball. You'll hear more later about how the financial support for college that my dad had promised me never materialized, so now I had only myself to depend on. At that moment, I vowed to use the same principles of training, development, and study that brought me success in athletics to create a similar level of financial success in business. These principles would come in handy again when I pursued my passion for learning spirituality, holistic thinking, and Eastern philosophies, culminating in my master's degree. I'm nothing if not intensely curious, persistent, and driven in competition with myself, with a side of humble :-) cockiness.

Like many of us, once I reached adulthood, I knew that if I mimicked the patterns of my family of origin, I would eventually end up being like them. There were some patterns I wanted to repeat, like the large extended family my grandparents created, a strong work ethic, and the Christian values central to the community I grew up in. There were also patterns of abuse, abandonment and resentment that I wanted to completely transcend.

In the last quarter-century, I feel honored to have coached twenty-three seasons of baseball, basketball, football and lacrosse, gone to the park with my kids, and on nearly every class field trip and chaperoned so, so many science camps! My wife and I have created dream family vacations, world travel, and the shared hobby of belonging to a Sand Dune Cult of social misfit ATV-riding bandits. This time spent with my children and adopted extended family is what makes my life extraordinary to me. It's not so much that we got to do all this cool stuff, but it's the people and relationships we have built and the lives we have shared.

I definitely made a better Butterfly Effect.

TESTED BY FIRE. FORGED IN FAITH.

My wife and I toured the Giant Sequoias in Yosemite for our twenty-sixth anniversary. We learned that the reason those trees are so rare is because they need fire. What!? Giant Sequoia cones are serotinous, meaning that fire on the forest floor causes them to dry out, open up, and release their seeds. In the early twentieth century, we started suppressing forest fires in the U.S. because of devastating fires like the "Big Blowup" in Idaho, Montana, and Washington in 1910, and also to protect timber resources. Seemed like good reasons at the time, yet suppressing forest fires also affected the giant redwood population. They need the fire to reproduce, to exist.

I've always had an affinity for trees. The Central Valley is all about agriculture, and trees were a dominant part of things growing up. My first business was selling walnuts I'd gathered. Learning this fact about the great Sequoias made me wonder if I am like them—tested by fire and forged in faith.

Maybe I've needed the "fire" to open myself and produce anew.

Experience has shown me nature's path. And rather humorously, and to my embarrassment, I don't always stay on that path! But here's what I know: **When I choose to follow the patterns that fuel nature's creative force, I have the potential to soar to unbelievable heights of service and healing of others.**

INNERCHAPTER

WE BE TREES!

(Nature as our guide)

Central to ecological approaches is the notion that our present environmental crisis is due primarily to a fractured worldview, which drastically separates mind and body, subject and object, culture and nature, thoughts and things, values and facts, spirit and matter, human and non-human.

This worldview is dualistic, mechanistic, atomistic, anthropocentric, and pathologically hierarchical. It unnecessarily elevates humans above the rest of the fabric of reality, alienating men and women from the intricate web of patterns and relationships that constitute the very nature of life, earth, and cosmos.

What's required to heal the planet we call home is to replace the fractured worldview we inherited with one that is more holistic, relational, integrative, Earth-honoring, and less arrogantly human-centered. This worldview honors the entire web of life, which has intrinsic value in and of itself—and a web that, not incidentally, is the bone and marrow of our existence.

Nature is a great teacher. Think like Nature in the process of becoming what you are capable of being,

Trees, a profound metaphor for life, symbolize growth and resilience. They anchor their roots deep into the earth to withstand storms and harsh conditions, just as we reach down and develop inner strength to navigate life's adversities. The seasonal cycles of shedding, budding, blooming, and seeding of leaves reflect the natural ebb and flow of our lives—change and renewal, birth and death.

Trees symbolize interconnectedness and community. Amazingly, tree scientists have discovered something fascinating about trees over the last few decades: **Trees live in community.** They share resources through their intertwining roots and communicate through a network of mycorrhizal connections called the "Woodwide Web." Their mutual support system, sharing resources, the old helping the young, the strong helping the weak so all can thrive, is a powerful metaphor for the value of relationships and community in human life.

Trees are one of the most mentioned living things in the Bible besides "man" and "God." Jeremiah urges all believers to be like a tree (17:7):

> "But blessed is the one who trusts in the Lord,
>   whose confidence is in him.
> They will be like a tree planted by the water
>   that sends out its roots by the stream.
> It does not fear when heat comes;
>   its leaves are always green.
> It has no worries in a year of drought
>   and never fails to bear fruit."

Scripture portrays trees continuously as things that communicate. Trees shout for joy in 1 Chronicles 16:33, clap their hands in Isaiah 55:12. They even argue in Judges 9:7–15. This pattern is especially odd because creatures that we would ordinarily think do communicate, like fish or birds, are never shown to speak in the Bible.

CHAPTER ONE

SPIRITUAL LENS— PICTURE POSSIBILITY

Seeing the parts. Seeing the whole. Seeing with energy.

A s soon as someone says the word *spiritual,* all kinds of things come up for people! Based on their religion, childhood, politics, personal traumas, or epiphanies, everybody has a reaction. It gets complicated, like a pizza with every topping known to humanity on it.

My take is simple: **Spirituality is a whole-body experience, not just a mental construct.** It's "seeing" and "being" within a spaciousness that is beyond all distinctions of good, bad, right, or wrong. Yet everything exists because of that space—pure consciousness aware of itself!

And I've always wondered: *What would it be like to have an intimate relationship with that spaciousness beyond all distinction?*

Have I lost you already? I'll let Deepak Chopra explain the beauty and vastness of this idea...

"Let's take just one example, the act of breathing. With every breath, **you inhale 10 to the 22nd power of atoms from the universe** [emphasis mine]; this astronomical volume of raw material enters your body from your environment and quickly becomes the cells of your heart, bones, kidneys, and liver. Then, with every exhaled breath, you release the same number of atoms from every part of your body. You're literally breathing out bits and pieces of your heart and kidneys."

He goes on to say that, therefore, we could be sharing our atoms with someone else at any given time—not just with people around us but with everyone who ever lived.

A human is not a static meat suit with a supercomputer brain running the show, somehow connected to an airy-fairy soul ready to ascend to a cloud in heaven when the meter on the meat suit runs out. We are a dynamic part of the whole universe, constantly exchanging molecules and subatomic particles with every organism that ever existed. It's science.

> "Humankind has not woven the web of life. We are but one thread within it. Whatever we do to the web, we do to ourselves. All things are bound together. All things connect."
>
> —*Chief Seattle, Leader of the Squamish and Duwamish Native American Tribes (quote discovered on the back of a wine bottle at Picayune Cellars & Mercantile, Calistoga, CA)*

So, why would it be so unusual to see ourselves in relationship with the spaciousness of everything and, at the same time, connected within ourselves in ways we never imagined? **The purpose of the Spiritual Lens is to practice seeing through a mind-body-energy connection,** a foundational aspect of developing a Whole Person Paradigm.

St. Francis of Assisi implores us to "start by doing what's necessary; then do what's possible, and suddenly you are doing the impossible." You connect your physical and spiritual self by engaging your body in spiritual practices—as simple as how you show up every day.

CULTIVATING YOUR SPIRITUAL LENS

Pursuing spiritual enlightenment knows no geographic or cultural boundaries. Looking through the Spiritual Lens is fundamentally a journey of the human spirit, seeking unity and understanding in a complex world.

The mind is a mirror of our awareness. A mirror reflects everything without judgment or attachment, just as the mind should be a clear, unbiased observer of our experiences. However, the mind has (as we know too well) distractions, negative emotions, and attachments which can cloud the mind's mirror-like nature, like specks of dust. Learning about our inner selves allows us to identify and remove these impediments, like dusting off a mirror with a little Windex to make the surface shiny and clear.

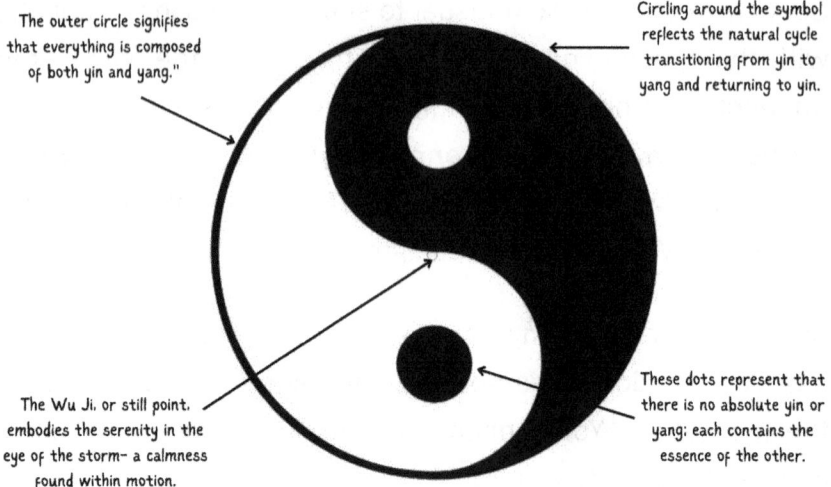

One of my favorite symbols is the taijitu or yin-yang image, showing how opposite forces—light and dark, male and female—are two sides of one principle. It represents the opposite but interconnected, self-perpetuating cycle of energy. Each contains the seed of its opposite within itself. **These forces can be considered complementary rather than opposing, interacting to form a dynamic system where the whole is greater than the assembled parts.**

What does this mean to you and me? The mind as a mirror demonstrates the yin and yang principle in action. Knowing others and knowing yourself—people think of these as different, independent things. In fact, they are different facets of the same thing and are intimately interconnected.

It's impossible to truly know other people without knowing yourself. As you mirror your own thoughts, you project them onto someone else, as they are projecting their mirror's reflection onto you. It's a cyclical effect.

Understanding this principle can do a lot to explain the relationships we have in our lives and how they serve us (or not!). We'll be working with this interconnectedness throughout the book.

> "Knowing others is wisdom; knowing yourself is Enlightenment."
>
> —*Chinese philosopher Lao Tzu*

What happens when we project our minds onto everything around us? How can we develop the awareness that it is even happening?

We can break it out into what you might call a step-by-step expansion: **seeing the parts, seeing the whole, seeing with energy.** This practice challenges all limits to the potential of an individual's life. How exciting is that?!

Seeing the parts is seeing a situation or problem and sorting out the different solutions. Humans have an incredible faculty for thinking critically and analyzing logically. Your mind-body connection enables you to think, observe, discern, and question what comes into your view and make decisions about those things, often in a split second!

Seeing the whole is the realization that your worldview isn't only what you inherited in your many years of life. Your worldview has actually been inherited for thousands of years. This level of awareness expands your perspective almost limitlessly, doesn't it? It opens up multiple cognitive lenses through which to see your life, and many possibilities you can choose from those lenses.

My wife and I went to Canyon Ranch one weekend for a spiritual retreat. We signed up for classes like sacred massage, walking meditation, and drumming. We thought the drumming class would be a kind of spiritual, shamanic experience and were really looking forward to it.

When we entered the room, it didn't look anything like what we expected—everybody was wearing sleek, colorful aerobic workout clothes. Kettlebells and Pilates balls were strewn all over, a boombox was belting out energetic music, and an impossibly fit person was revving up the group with her headset microphone.

It was a Jazzercise class! There were drums, but... no Birkenstocks (except for my Birks), peaceful contemplation, or anything that resembled what we were here for.

We were used to a paradigm and made the assumption that drumming was a ritual, while there were clearly other perspectives on that. Lesson learned!

Another expansion of your Spiritual Lens is to see yourself as part of something bigger than yourself—in terms of connection with others, connection with nature, and connection with a whole that is spacious and beyond definition or bounds. You realize that we aren't really separate; we are connected. You begin to see yourself *as a connection* and to see reality as an undivided whole.

Back in his day, my grandfather didn't have the benefit of emotional intelligence training, vision quest retreats, and weekends with Western-trained shamans. To him, a "retreat" was a military last resort! Today, there's so much research we can access and so many different techniques.

Think of the potential you can reach in your life. What problems would you be able to solve? What could you accomplish by yourself, and what could you accomplish with other passionate people? Maybe one person can't effect change, but how about the connections and collective power of others?

These questions speak to the real purpose of spiritual growth: **To create things that are enduring and that elevate the human spirit.**

Seeing with energy involves the patterns and everything that connects everything to everything, and how it occurs for you. It's not just the content you are seeing; it's the energy that connects all those 10^{22} molecules, if you will. When you see with energy, you are moving beyond the constructs of good and bad, right and wrong—and you are at one with that which is always there and that which is what "all" is.

My colleague, John Allen Mollenhauer (JAM), is a leading Performance Lifestyle® Coach and the founder of Regenus

Center, along with his partner and wife, Mariahna Suzan. Here is how he describes energy: "It's defined in physics as the 'capacity to do work,' but energy is more than that. Energy meets your capacity and enables you to expand and develop it. But to do that, you need to managesource, enhance the production of and harness energy proactively. And never has that been more important than right now."

As you might imagine, it's a matter of faith. Ah, another tricky word that means different things to different people. Have you noticed how often "faith" is used in the popular context as a synonym for "superstition"? I'll simplify it as this powerful concept: **Faith is believing you can make a difference and then actually doing something to make that difference—and eventually becoming the difference you want to make.**

How does that sound?

The Apostle Paul emphasized the importance of faith when he wrote, "We walk by faith, not by sight" (2 Corinthians 5:7). Faith, coupled with seeing through a Spiritual Lens, enables us to perceive the interconnectedness of all things, transcending the material world. In this context, or at least through my own Spiritual Lens, faith does NOT mean religion, and one type of faith is not better or worse than another. It's *an intrinsic sense of hope that everyone has inside*, ready for them to discover and use, and make a difference in small or massive ways.

> "People who have faith in life are like swimmers who entrust themselves to a rushing river. They neither abandon themselves to its current nor try to resist it. Rather, they adjust their every movement to the watercourse, use it with purpose and skill, and enjoy the adventure."
>
> —Brother David Steindl-Rast

When you see the energy and interconnectedness of all things within your spiritual vision, you become like Brother David's swimmers, who trust themselves to the rushing river of everyday life. You have faith that you have possibilities for days—as far as your imagination can take you!

So, let's talk about possibilities ...

> "Don't judge each day by the harvest you reap but by the seeds you plant."
>
> —Robert Louis Stevenson

The work of planting the seeds for what is possible starts here, through the Spiritual Lens. You look at **who you are and what your potential REALLY means**. You have the design and a potentiality, like the seed or acorn that becomes a tree. It just needs to be energized by the heavens and nourished by the earth.

> **The first graduate-level class I took was Holistic Nutrition,** taught by an Acupuncturist from Oakland. She started the class by telling a story about developing a relationship with plants.

I sat at my desk, thinking, *I'm paying good money for this school. I have three kids and a mortgage. Are we REALLY talking about making friends with plants??* As she told of her meditative walks around her neighborhood, she passed around a vibrant green clip of fresh rosemary and asked us all to experience it with as many of our senses as we could.

The smell and texture of the rosemary were extraordinary, and I started to soften my rigid ideas about what a holistic nutrition class should be about. What was powerful was the space she created for us to actuate ALL the senses, which is precisely what I did—an *aha* moment for me!

She went on to explain how rosemary is a potent medicinal herb with a seven-thousand-year history. She listed some of the uses of the plant, like improved digestion, boosting the immune system, increasing brain function, and detoxing the liver. Its essential oils contain important components such as α-terpineol, α-pinene, cineol, camphene, borneol, and bornyl acetate. Fresh rosemary has very high levels of vitamins A, C, B6, thiamin, and folate. It also has minerals like iron, calcium and magnesium. Rosemary has plenty of antioxidants, including diterpenes, carnosol, and rosmarinic acid (RA). Rosemary is also a beautiful plant that, in climates like California, grows into rich green, fragrant hedges. Wow!

This class taught me to see things more through the lens of nature. I grew to accept that developing relationships with plants might be something worth exploring, and I was reminded again of my intimate love of trees.

Today, I enjoy saying *hi* to the rosemary plants in our neighborhood during my morning walks. Sometimes, I break off a twig and vigorously rub the green needles between my palms to intensify the aroma. And take a giant inhale... aaah...

SEE YOUR SUPER BOWL THROUGH THE SPIRITUAL LENS

Wait, where did the Super Bowl come into all this? Weren't we just talking about seeds and plants? Hey, hear me out! The Super Bowl is an iconic sports event that probably every kid who plays football dreams about. Some of my favorite stories are of people who spent their whole lives trying to get to the Super Bowl and never made it—yet. They still ended up having a great and memorable life. And people keep dreaming about it and trying for it.

In our lives, there will always be something like the Super Bowl to dream about or aspire to. This is a good thing. Living through the Spiritual Lens allows us to dream and aspire, yet with a clear picture of how things fall into place in the universe, who we are in it, and what part WE play in it. Those are the things that will give us a great life, whether we ever go to the Super Bowl (or reach Nirvana or ...).

The Whole Person Paradigm is not about results; it's about process.

I love to make what's impossible possible, and what's invisible visible. So, let's start to bring in the THPM to help visualize the human gifts that are associated with your Spiritual Lens and affirmations to offer for each. Notice if you accept, reject, adapt, or want to expand any of them to suit you. They represent uncommon ways of seeing things, and a little discomfort is a hopeful reaction.

The sides of the Spiritual Lens triangle represent your uniquely human gifts of *self-awareness*, *sensation of the six senses*, and *sense of humor*. Developing the Spiritual Lens of self-awareness, the physical sensation of what that feels like, and the humility (through humor and fun) to accept not having everything all figured out—this blows the lid off what is possible!

Self-awareness. This is the cornerstone of spiritual fitness. It's not just knowing your autobiography or genealogy, and it goes beyond being aware of your expertise and talents. It is not just identifying what you like or don't like. **Self-awareness is discovering who and what you really are.**

Developing this gift helps you see the parts, see the whole, and see with energy through your Spiritual Lens. You examine your thoughts and actions critically (yet without judgment). You notice the reality of the mirror of your mind. You begin to open the lens to observe different worldviews.

Through introspection, you gain insights into your nature, as well as your place in the spaciousness of existence. It's a deeply personal practice, humbling and exciting. Sometimes you pray for people, and sometimes people pray for you. You find, somewhat counterintuitively, strength through weakness.

Let's hold up a minute. A younger me would NEVER believe that I could have written what you just read, and even as I write this, I'm getting emotional about my own experience with this idea. In my late forties, I bought a twenty-one-day devotional book, the kind of practice that includes a daily message, prayer, meditation and fasting. (I have to laugh now because it took me forty days to complete!)

One day, I read: *"Sometimes you pray for people, and sometimes people pray for you."* That statement stopped me in my tracks. *What are they talking about? I'm independent. I take care of everyone else. I don't need anybody's effing help or prayers!*

It was a humbling *aha* moment for me. The fact was this: I didn't always like being that way. A small part of me resented that I had to be responsible for everybody else, and I realized I DID need effing help. My epiphany was that this wasn't a weakness but a strength, a gift to myself and the people helping me!

From a self-awareness perspective, I learned to be grateful and willing to ask for help and to actively ask for prayers. Now, I know for a fact that I am surrounded and held by the energy of other people's prayers and love for me.

Self-awareness affirmations:

1. I choose to stand apart from my thoughts or feelings and examine or change them (if necessary).
2. I am aware of the way I think about things and how it impacts my attitudes, behaviors, and the results I'm getting in my life.
3. I am aware of a difference between my biological, genealogical, psychological, and sociological scripting—and my own deep inner presence.
4. When someone's response to what I say or do challenges the way I see myself, I choose to evaluate the feedback against deep personal self-knowledge and learn from that.

> "Real religion transforms anxiety into laughter."
> —Alan Watts

Sense of Humor. A sense of humor encourages you to approach life with levity. A humorous perspective allows you to detach from your ego and the trivialities of existence.

This spiritual stuff can get heady sometimes; after all, it's about our very lives and the foundation of existence. And remember ALL those reactions people can have around their ideas on spirituality? **Humor creates a space where you can talk about things that are serious or complex,** to agree that, in essence, they're still constructs packed with paradox and perfidy.

Does it feel to you like "spiritual" and "humor" don't belong in the same sentence (or even the same world)? Some people feel that way, that enlightenment comes from sober, sacrificial, "holy" behavior. I say the Spiritual Lens—all the lenses, for that matter—exist in the yin and yang of our existence. We live in the world with the good, the bad, the sacred, and the ugly, and all are here for our lessons and development. Humor plays a huge role in the Whole Person Paradigm.

One of my favorite shows is *South Park* because it's funny, brings out my off-color side, and is so offensive that it can talk about issues like racism, politics and religion. Many of us can watch the show and laugh at ourselves. I'm a big fan of Jesus, and they have some fun with that, too (it's not really about what Jesus represents; it's more about the people around him). And I wonder what the Laughing Buddha is always laughing about. He's not even the real Buddha, but a mixed-up interpretation of examples of Buddha nature.

Humor can be good or it can suck. It takes self-awareness to understand and use humor for its positive gifts. Such as:

- Providing perspective and balance in discussions and debates.
- Diffusing tension, lightening the mood, and preventing conversations from becoming overly intense or polarized.
- Inviting a more open and relaxed atmosphere, which can foster better communication and understanding.
- Helping us enjoy seeing the world differently, make unexpected connections, think creatively, and spark innovative approaches to problem-solving.

- Building bridges between people by helping to communicate ideas effectively and increasing interest in the topic.
- Making information more relatable and memorable, promoting greater understanding and participation.
- Creating camaraderie and fostering connections among individuals. It can unite people in shared experiences and build relationships based on mutual understanding and laughter. Humor can help bridge gaps and overcome differences, promoting unity and community.

You can tell I like humor. What can I say? It's funny!

Caveat: **Exercising sensitivity and tact when using humor is vital.** Humor can deeply hurt someone's feelings, whether or not it was meant to. Levity should never undermine the gravity of a subject or be used to dismiss or trivialize essential issues or people.

Sense of humor affirmations:

1. I can laugh at myself.
2. I don't struggle for perfection, and I realize that my mistakes are the only thing I can truly call my own.
3. I use humor to embrace my own humanness and share it with others.
4. I look for ways to turn lemons into lemonade through the creative force of humor and to integrate learning experiences.

Sensation of the Six Senses. We have natural sensory signals in our bodies, giving us the ability to perceive movement, position, and physical sensations (kinesthetics). We have our five senses of sight, hearing, touch, smell and taste, and what we call our sixth sense—intuition. By the way, I'm just using "sixth" as more than five; there could be infinitely more. I'll stick with six; you're welcome to prove there are others!

The act of moving our bodies helps energy flow through and around us. Sensory bodily awareness shows us, in every moment, that the mind is not separate from the body. Our physical sensations often mirror our mental state and offer us clues as to what we should be aware of in terms of our feelings, emotions and thoughts (such as those creating dust on our mental mirrors like an unwashed car window!).

Kinesthetic learning is shown to bolster cognitive, social, and emotional development. Many people learn and embed information more effectively when they can move their bodies and interact with their environments (learning on the job, for example, typically leads to faster promotions). It's all connected and useful to us.

- **Use your six senses** to fully experience the moment, object, person, or situation. Like me, with the fresh rosemary, smelling it the first time and now regularly as a ritual, you heighten your self-awareness and raise your appreciation and joy. Using your sight through your Spiritual Lens sharpens your view and discernment. Tapping into your intuition/sixth sense amplifies the messages that will develop your self-awareness.

- **Move your body** through physical activity and practices like yoga, strength training and martial arts. You can literally raise your spirits and clear your mind through the release of endorphins and serotonin, which will sharpen your senses and spiritual vision—and it's fun! Your awareness of your body helps you maintain an energetic balance. Use your body to physically enjoy and embed an experience. It will be much more powerful and lasting in your memory.

- **Listen to what your body is telling you.** In Taoism and Chinese medicine, the axiom is: The *qi* (energy) flows where the mind goes. In other words, your attention focuses your life energy—you are in the driver's seat! When you become aware of input or circumstances that cloud your mind, you are developing the ability to work with that awareness to learn their lessons and move into a better space.

Sensation of six senses affirmations:

1. I am aware of my body and energetic field and proactively seek energetic balance.
2. I am aware of the patterns and connections between the other gifts and what they feel like through all my senses.
3. I proactively train my body in multiple ways for fitness, recreation, and experiencing joy.
4. I am aware of how my moods, energy, and effectiveness in every other area of my human intelligence are connected to the sensations of the six senses.

MATERIALISTIC AND HOLISTIC PARADIGMS: TWO SIDES OF ALL THE COINS

We start with the idea that your worldview creates the realm of what's possible for you. We've been used to looking at this through the "materialist paradigm" lens—the concept that everything, including mental events, is composed of physical matter; therefore, everything can be quantified. This paradigm has its place—but this is a slippery slope.

Purely mechanistic and scientific worldviews leave out the human concepts of soul and spirit, reducing all experience to a deterministic chemical stew. On the opposite end of the spectrum, some religious worldviews leave out essential parts of science that they believe don't fit with their interpretation of wisdom traditions.

The "holistic paradigm" attempts to include both, without reducing the value of one over the other or keeping them conveniently separate in case they conflict or don't "conform." We want a system that is expressive rather than sacrificial. The Tao of Pizza promotes practice as a holistic approach to self-awareness and spiritual fitness.

The best of both worlds—literally! A holistic worldview opens us up to unlimited self-knowledge and imagination. We create opportunities for innovative, inclusive, and regenerative solutions.

Many people are sensing a growing reconciliation between Science and Spirituality and the birth of a *new worldview that has the potential to radically transform what it means to be human.* Vastly expanded possibilities for spiritual experiences exist in this new paradigm.

KNOT KNOWING VS. NOT KNOWING

In Boy Scouts (which I flunked out of by the time I was ten and got a real job), we'd go on camping trips, where they would teach us how to tie all of these wonderfully useful knots. With some practice, you could learn them well enough to tie one without even thinking about it. When you could do that, you were in the zone!

Well, it's also easy enough to practice thoughts (whether true or not true) so much that they develop into patterns of thought that lead to knee-jerk reactions. Before you know it, you are someone who believes you can never go to college because no one in your family ever has; that nobody will EVER walk or bike instead of driving an EV; that some humans have smaller brains than other humans. Or you're like this lady...

> **"It is narrated that in the 1870s,** an old lady—a very devout Methodist—moved to Colchester to a house in the neighborhood of The City Road, in London, where mistaking the Hall of Science for a chapel, she sat at the feet of Charles Bradlaugh (a famous atheist who founded the secular society in England in 1866) for many years, entranced by his eloquence, without questioning his orthodoxy or moulting a feather of her faith. I fear I shall be defrauded from my just martyrdom in the same way."

What's happening is that you are also seeing a distorted worldview and need to swipe clean your Spiritual Lens. Like knot knowing, it is easy to stay stuck in those thoughts and beliefs until you don't think at all; it becomes a simple reaction, whether true or false, helpful or harmful.

> "The perfect man uses his mind as a mirror; it grasps nothing, refuses nothing, receives but does not keep."
>
> —Chuang Tzu

The Greatest Slice

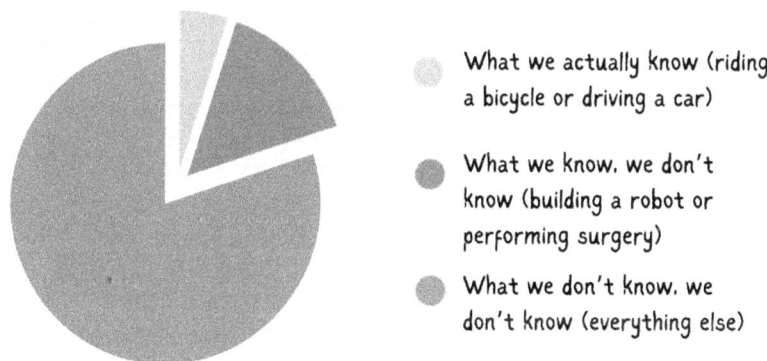

- What we actually know (riding a bicycle or driving a car)
- What we know, we don't know (building a robot or performing surgery)
- What we don't know, we don't know (everything else)

The truth about worldview is that the actual slice for "what we know" is so infinitesimally small that we wouldn't actually be able to represent it on the chart (or taste it in the pizza!). And even the medium slice will be pretty small compared to "what we don't know that we don't know"—because that's infinity! The purpose of this chart is to bring home this perception to help you become comfortable with *Not Knowing* and to realize our distorted view. The "perfect man (person)," as Chuang Tzu describes it, uses their mind as a mirror, refuses nothing, and receives everything without attachment.

Your spiritual fitness self-awareness practice will get you to the intentional state of *Not Knowing* so you can be free from the perceptual and functional constraints of materialistic small thinking.

The more you open yourself up to the pleasures of Not Knowing, the more you will... know! And the most exciting part? It will expand your "experience" of what you don't know you don't know, which is the most important pizza slice in the Tao of Pizza.

THE PAYOFF

Exercise your Spiritual Intelligence muscle! You can "work out" when you're by yourself, with family and friends, or as a leader in your business. Essentially...

Spiritual Intelligence means cultivating unconditional love. This is not an easy state to achieve or maintain, but the practice itself is crucial and rewarding.

> "To love without condition, to talk without intention, to give without reason and to care without expectation; that's the spirit of true love."
>
> —*Unknown*

When cultivated and applied effectively, spiritual intelligence can contribute to addressing some of our most pressing problems in so many ways, such as:

- Foster a worldview and value system that promotes cooperation, empathy, and a deeper understanding of the interconnectedness of all living beings, which will increase collaboration across diverse groups and perspectives to find holistic solutions.
- Promote continuous self-reflection and personal growth, which leads to taking responsibility for one's actions and seeking to change behaviors that contribute to societal problems.
- Guide important decision-making in various fields, including business, politics and government.
- Encourage people to develop a deep sense of compassion and empathy for others. This can lead to more inclusive and compassionate approaches to addressing social and humanitarian issues like poverty, inequality, and discrimination.
- See the long-term consequences of actions and decisions and highlight our responsibility for the well-being of humanity and the planet. This can motivate us to make more sustainable and forward-thinking solutions to climate change and resource depletion.
- Equip individuals with conflict resolution tools that prioritize understanding, forgiveness and reconciliation, which can help resolve disputes and promote peace in interpersonal and international contexts.

- Provide access to a greater capacity to cope with adversity and maintain a sense of hope and purpose during challenging times.
- Cultivate spiritual intelligence that will improve mental and emotional well-being, reducing the negative impacts of stress and anxiety.

Sincere collaboration and dialogue among diverse perspectives are crucial to helping all humans become spiritually fit and to finding inclusive and effective solutions to complex global challenges.

HERE'S THE (INTER)CONNECTION

This story, coming out of my backyard, is, to me, a perfect testament to how a holistic approach based on spiritual intelligence can address a pressing and complex societal problem...

Napa, California, a world-class travelers' destination (and my current home), lies in the flood-prone valley of the Napa River. Over three decades, nineteen floods have cost residents their homes, enormous economic losses, environmental damage, and loss of human lives. The river is the second largest confluence in the San Francisco Bay and represents one of the top five biodiversity hotspots in the world!

The Napa River curves and turns in a kind of oxbow shape, each part supporting mini-biomes of land and aquatic life (for example, a rare breeding ground for steelhead trout). The U.S. Army Corps of Engineers proposed solving the flood issue by "straightening out" the river via a canal built through the middle of town—expedient but a non-starter for local leaders, residents, and environmental groups such as the Friends of the Napa River (a group I volunteered for).

In 1998, a ballot measure approved Napa's "Living River Flood Protection Project," forming an almost unheard-of partnership between Napa's flood control and water conservation district, the U.S. Army Corps of Engineers and environmental groups, with the ambitious plan to return the Napa River to its natural floodplain with its unique diversity of aquatic life. It was a formidable, eleven-billion-dollar undertaking, where diverse communities came together, partnering with government, to mitigate floods while restoring and protecting critical ecosystems. No canal was built; the Napa River remains in its natural state!

The Living River Flood Project experience is inherently spiritual, a shining example of how spiritual intelligence can be embodied in a large-scale initiative based on the commitment to a higher purpose where human well-being and environmental health are intertwined.

The way this project was carried out exemplifies compassion, ethics, collaboration, and a forward-thinking approach to environmental stewardship.

This is Spiritual Intelligence. This is looking at the world through the Spiritual Lens.

> "The individual is the aperture through which the whole energy of the universe is aware of itself."
>
> —Alan Watts

WRAPPIN' IT UP

What you are is the Ground of Being, the intelligent energy of the universe. THAT is reality! The practice of focusing your attention on what you really are (which is not at all who you think you are) provides access to the *actual* experience of BEing.

I saw a t-shirt that read: "We are all stars." We are beings that use solar radiation from the sun to generate a human. That's a pretty amazing and simple truth.

This chapter, the Spiritual Lens, sets the stage for the rest of the book, which will offer loads more truth bombs, personal practices, and techniques that will help you observe the mirror of your mind, raise your spiritual intelligence, and embody your worldview from a place of functional and perceptual freedom.

In the final analysis, remember this: Enjoy the simplicity and lightness of being in the world through the Spiritual Lens. **You don't have to go and figure everything out!** As a matter of fact, if you did figure everything out and know it all, life basically would kind of suck, if you know what I mean...that would be a world that lacks true wonder.

There's one thing that all true spirituality has in common, whether derived from faith, science, nature, or the arts. And that is a sense of wonder and love.

It's a lifetime process. Have some fun with it. Speaking of fun, the next chapter attempts to put the FUN in fundamentals.

> "Perhaps we'll never know how far the path can go, how much a human being can truly achieve, until we realize that the ultimate reward is not a gold medal but the path itself."
>
> —George Leonard

GOING DEEPER

Write down three things you learned from this chapter, and one big AHA!

NOTES

INNERCHAPTER
TETRAHIDDLE-HADDLE HOLISTIC PARADIGM MODEL
(Time for Arts & Crafts!)

Remember the kick-ass (another word for integrative) arts and crafts guide I promised? Here it is! I'm going to teach you how to build the THPM in order to visualize how it works, how the triangles (Lenses) fit together, and how each edge of the triangles relates to the other.

You're going to build the model with your bare hands for the ultimate sensory learning experience. (Or you could do a cold plunge in 35-55-degree water for three minutes—both practices will engage the sensation of your six senses sufficiently to heighten your self-awareness.)

Equipment:

- The colors you selected for your six gifts. If you haven't done it, do it now!
- Three colored pencils, straws, or other kinds of sticks or tubes that will represent the sides of a triangle.
- Rubber bands, paper clips, strings, or another creative way to connect the sides of the triangle.

Instructions: Using your Spiritual Lens as the first triangle, construct it as you see in the illustration, using your color-coded "gifts" as the edges of the triangle. Now, hold your Spiritual Lens in your hands, and state what you would do if you knew you couldn't fail. Take a stand for what is possible for you. It's beyond your wildest imagination. Notice how you can see yourself—and the world—through a Spiritual Lens.

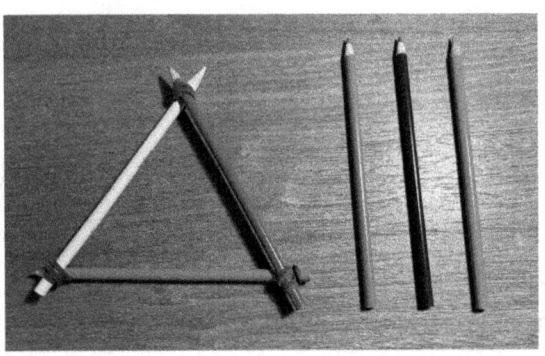

Speaking of imagination, now grab the colors you chose for *imagination* and *inner voice*. Create the Emotional Lens triangle by adding these two edges to the *Sensation of the six senses*. The Emotional Lens shares the edge of the sensation of the six senses because our Spiritual and Emotional Lenses include the direct experience of our sensory life.

One of the beauties of a tetrahedral model is a physical representation of the relationship between the sides and how all four sides share a common edge. Each side, or lens in our case, is in relationship to each of the other lenses. The shared edges are significant.

The last gift to be added to the model is *choice*. It completes the Mental Lens and Action Lens triangles at the same time (check out the illustration). The Mental Lens shares the *imagination* edge with the Emotional Lens, and the third edge of the Mental Lens is *self-awareness*. As you engage with each chapter, the relationship between developing your gifts and expanding your lenses will become clearer.

The Action Lens pivots on the *choice* edge. And the other two edges are *inner voice* and *humor*. After all, action is a choice to follow your inner voice, and humor creates the space for trying new things and looking goofy at first.

You are now holding a model of the Whole Person Paradigm! You are the space within, and the edges have no boundaries. Therefore, neither do you! Read on to learn more about the interrelationship of the lenses and gifts, and how you can apply this whole-person perspective to practice BEing a path to peace and prosperity.

CHAPTER TWO

EMOTIONAL LENS—PASSION
Principles of pursuit

The thoughts and beliefs we experience through our Spiritual Lens trigger energetic patterns of self-reinforcing emotions and actions.** The highest expression of those patterns is unconditional love.

Our thoughts and beliefs are our internal narratives about ourselves, others, and the world around us. They can be conscious or subconscious and are influenced by our past experiences, cultural backgrounds, and personal values. Intense emotional experiences create patterned reactions that are energetically imprinted onto our senses as emotions.

Emotions are something we physically feel. Most people consider them "in your head." THEY ARE NOT. From the folks at Authenticity Associates Coaching & Counseling: "What we think of as emotion is the experience of **energy moving through the body.** This is generally felt as sensations of contraction, such as tension, or expansion, such as calm. The Latin derivative for the word emotion, *emotere*, literally means "energy in motion."

Embodied energy shapes our perception of events. We form a meaning or understanding of what is happening in that event—positive, negative, or neutral. Our interpretation triggers an emotional response in our body that is sometimes so strong it becomes a knee-jerk reaction. If we interpret a situation as threatening, we may experience fear, anxiety, or anger. If we see a situation as positive or rewarding, we may feel joy, excitement, passion, or hope.

This is our Emotional Lens—the basis of how our internal narrative sees our world.

Our Emotional Lens can reinforce our initial thoughts and beliefs in a kind of feedback loop: Our thoughts and beliefs trigger emotions => which influence our actions => the outcomes of our actions further validate our initial thoughts and beliefs => which strengthens the energetic biological pattern => which comes into play when we encounter a "triggering" situation.

As you can probably guess, this self-reinforcing cycle can have both positive and negative patterns—and positive or negative consequences.

At eighteen years old, I found myself perched high in the air, clutching two hefty roof beams thirty feet above the ground. I was unsteadily standing on a makeshift scaffolding of scrap wood. My uncle, a seasoned carpenter, hammered nails into the beams with a confidence that was nothing short of awe-inspiring. We were framing the roof of a quaint downtown home in the Land Park area of Sacramento, and the pressure to get it right was intense.

Then... I made the cardinal error of looking down at the ground below. My heart started racing, and an image of plummeting from this height coursed through my mind. Fear gripped me. My legs began to shake uncontrollably, threatening to betray me. I felt sweat bead on my forehead.

Evidently sensing my turmoil, my uncle burst out with a hearty laugh that reverberated through the neighborhood. A mixture of amusement and camaraderie, maybe; to me, it felt like mockery. I got really pissed! Anger surged through me, momentarily eclipsing my fear. I clenched my teeth, resenting my uncle's cavalier demeanor in the face of such danger. *What the *expletive* is this guy thinking? He's laughing when I'm about to fall to my death!*

To be continued...

Emotions can be powerful motivators that drive us to engage in certain actions and avoid others as we go through our days, weeks, and entire lives. For example, when we feel confident and optimistic, we are more inclined to take risks, pursue opportunities, and live more passionately. When we feel anxious or fearful, we're more likely to avoid challenges, withdraw from situations, and see our life as a never-ending struggle.

MAKING THE INVISIBLE VISIBLE

> "Until you make the unconscious conscious, it will direct your life and you will call it fate."
>
> —*Carl Gustav Jung*

Most people think they are their thoughts. A man named Rene told us this about four hundred years ago, and we believed it. Sorry, suckers, we all fell for it! I had a T-shirt that read: *"I think, therefore I am."*

This is the biggest lie ever perpetrated on a species! If you think you are your thoughts, stop thinking. See how that goes. Your thoughts are going to keep thoughting. You are NOT your thoughts.

Why is this important? Because, as Carl Jung cautions, we can go through life unconscious of our emotions and their sometimes-destructive patterns, which then allows those emotions to jump into the driver's seat of our subconscious. We accept that we ARE our thoughts, so we witlessly hand over the steering wheel and hold onto our hats!

Recognizing this self-reinforcing cycle is crucial to personal growth, self-awareness, and well-being. How do we do it? We want to bring the unconscious to the surface (the practices of spiritual fitness we saw in Chapter One help us do that). We then CHALLENGE and REFRAME negative or unhelpful emotional patterns by becoming aware of our thoughts, beliefs, and the sensations and feelings that accompany our emotions. Psychologists call this process *cognitive restructuring,* and in practice, find that this "reframing" can lead to more positive emotions, healthier behaviors, and a break from emotion-triggering patterns that may be holding us back.

My story continues...

> **The emotional rollercoaster I was riding seemed endless** until my inner voice broke through the chaos.
>
> It whispered to me, urging me to regain control and guiding me to stop and take a deep breath. I inhaled deeply from my belly and let it out slowly, feeling my center begin to settle down. I shifted my full focus on the task at hand, blocking out the dizzying view below. Slowly, the tremors in my legs subsided, and I steadied the beam with focus and determination.
>
> My uncle continued to nail in the beam, and the rhythm of our work returned. I marveled at how my emotions had transformed! Fear had given way to anger, and anger had been replaced by a calm

determination. The imagined fall was no longer the dominant thought in my mind; it was replaced by the drive to succeed.

With each precise swing of the hammer, the house's framework grew stronger. As the sun dipped below the horizon, I realized my emotions were like a storm that had passed, leaving a newfound strength and resilience behind. I had faced this fear, conquered my anger, and found my center high above the grassy lawn. In that moment, I experienced that emotions, like the roof beams I held, could be harnessed and channeled to achieve remarkable things.

I believe to this day that I was saved from a potentially nasty experience because I had learned the mind-body training of visualization as a teen, and my sports experience had taught me breathing techniques I was able to draw upon. I knew to listen to my inner voice so I could think clearly and refocus with strength.

Through the years, I've ultimately come to trust myself and my inner wisdom. I've slowly learned to differentiate between my inner voice and external influences, self-doubt, or other WMDs (Weapons of Mass Distraction) like social media and phone notifications.

EXPAND AND DEVELOP YOUR EMOTIONAL LENS

The sides of the Emotional Lens triangle in our Tetrahiddle-Haddle Model are *sensation of the six senses, imagination, and inner voice,* all of which can contribute significantly to developing our emotional capacity. We can harness these gifts to illuminate our path toward positive intentions and passionate, fulfilling living through attention and curiosity.

Sensation of the six senses. We introduced this gift in Chapter One. It can **influence emotions by providing feedback about your physical state and influencing your subjective experience.**

You can cultivate self-awareness by paying attention to your thoughts, feelings, and the messages you're given through your bodily sensations. Notice how you react in different situations and the ideas that will arise spontaneously. For instance, when you experience physical relaxation through activities like deep breathing, progressive muscle relaxation, or meditation, you feel calmer, and your stress or anxiety is reduced.

Similarly, when you engage in physical activities such as dancing, playing football, or hiking, you experience enhanced feelings of joy, excitement, well-being, and other positive sensations.

It's important to point out that our emotions and their relationship to the sensation of the six senses are billions of years old; however, our language and the mental constructs we use to describe them are only a few thousand years old.

Let's learn a new language!

Sensation of the six senses affirmations:

1. I am aware of my body and energetic field and proactively seek energetic balance.
2. I am aware of the patterns and connections between the other gifts and what they feel like through all my senses.
3. I proactively train my body in multiple ways for fitness, recreation, and experiencing joy.
4. I am aware of how my moods, energy and effectiveness in every other area of my human intelligence is connected to my kinesthetic experience.

Imagination. You have the natural ability to create mental images or scenarios not present in reality. It plays a pivotal role in *shaping your emotions by allowing you to simulate experiences and anticipate their potential outcomes*, whether positive and pleasant or negative and fearful. Imagination can intensify emotions by amplifying the sensory and cognitive aspects of an experience, even if it's not actually happening.

Imagination affirmations:

1. I think ahead.
2. I visualize my life beyond its present reality.
3. I use visualization to help reaffirm and realize my goals.
4. I look for new and creative ways to solve problems in a variety of situations and value the different views of others.

Inner voice. You have a gut-feeling consciousness that comes from an eternal place. It is NOT the random thoughts that swirl around in your head. Your inner voice is instinctive inner wisdom; *it senses the difference between social conditioning and natural principles.* It can reinforce or challenge your emotional states.

This is where self-talk comes in. You can train your inner voice through positive self-talk to shift your responses to a situation—to cultivate a growth mindset, boost confidence, and foster resilience. *Your inner voice is a powerful tool for emotional regulation and self-reflection.*

Inner voice affirmations:

1. I sometimes feel an inner prompting that I should do something or that I shouldn't do something I'm about to do.
2. I sense the difference between "social conscience"—what society has conditioned me to value—and my own inner directives.
3. I inwardly sense the reality of universal principles such as integrity and trustworthiness.
4. I see a pattern in human experience, bigger than the society in which I live, that validates the reality of principles.

Imagination, sensation of the six senses, and inner voice are superpowers developed by choice in order to have even greater choice.

They put you back at the wheel, in the driver's seat, goggles on and scarf to the wind!!

The story of me on that ladder shows how these three gifts work together with our Emotional Lens. I needed all three that crazy day. My imagination alone, with my emotions running amok and no inner voice, could have had me seeing and believing the worst-case scenario—and actually falling off the scrap-wood scaffolding to complete that picture in my mind. If I had my inner voice calling to me but no sense of my body, I might not have understood the signals I was getting that my emotions were running wild or been unable (or unwilling) to calm myself down. If my emotions kept running my imagination and bodily responses without my inner voice guiding me... another potential disaster!

But mind-body awareness kept my imagination in check. My sensation of the six senses of how my body was responding to all those emotions of anger, fear, etc., showed me the warning signs of collapse and allowed me to stand steadily. And my inner voice was there to say, *"You're gonna fall if you don't rein in your emotions. Take a breath, dude!"*

Teamwork for the win!

DASHIN' FOR PASSION

So, what about the "passion" in the chapter title?

I'm glad you asked!

Poet Linda Ellis invites: "Your life is made of two dates and a dash [on your tombstone]. Make the most of the dash."

What are you going to do with your dash?

My best friend has a tattoo that reads *memento mori*, a Marcus Aurelius adage that means this: *Remember, you're going to die.*

Sound morbid? I don't think so!

To me, it's an invitation, a challenge—even a mandate—to make the most of your one life. You have your superpowers (your birthright) at your disposal to authentically develop your capacity in all areas of your life. Zig Ziglar's Wheel of Life outlined those areas in a convenient (pizza) pie chart, which I hope will raise your creative and passionate appetite as you read on.

Zig Ziglar's Wheel of Life

Career, Financial, Spiritual, Physical, Intellectual, Family, Social

The secret "sauce" is **passion,** that strong, almost inexplicable feeling of enthusiasm, excitement, or irresistible impulse to do something. It's felt in the heart. It's always available to us to tap into. The kind of passion I'm talking about here is not an unhealthy internalized pressure or obsession. It is less about sexual passion or intimacy (albeit an important ingredient of a loving, fulfilling life) and more about **the energy we bring to everything we do in our lives—to make the most of our dash.**

The pizza "toppings" are the emotions that drive the whole delectable experience of pursuing your most audacious goals in body, mind and spirit.

Pushing the metaphor hopefully not too far... the essential ingredients that support the most delicious pizza (in other words, your passionate pursuits toward peace and prosperity) are:

1. **Emotional Intelligence**
2. **Intrinsic Motivation**
3. **Collaboration and Relationships**

Let's dive into each one ...

#1 EMOTIONAL INTELLIGENCE

We might call emotional intelligence the pizza crust—the foundation for all the other ingredients.

Emotional intelligence encompasses everything we've discussed so far in this chapter. It involves your awareness and understanding of your emotions, strengths, weaknesses, and triggers. It is the ability to regulate and manage your emotions. With strong emotional regulation skills, you can more effectively navigate setbacks, challenges, and failures. You are less likely to be discouraged or derailed by negative emotions and can bounce back to maintain your motivation, momentum, and passion.

Emotional intelligence influences self-efficacy, an individual's belief in their ability to accomplish tasks and achieve desired outcomes. People with high emotional intelligence can better recognize and build on their capabilities, which enhances their self-efficacy and just keeps getting better and better!

Important note: Not only does the emotionally intelligent individual understand their own emotions, but they also have a heightened sense of the emotions of the people around them.

#2 INTRINSIC MOTIVATION

We can be motivated by many things: fear, instant gratification, money, external rewards, and avoiding consequences. This kind of motivation is good in certain situations, yet in many cases, it's not helpful to a person in the long run. Why? Because we often tie our motivation to our *perception* of what the reward will be, which doesn't always materialize. Or we chase what are really *other people's* goals, not ours. Afterward, success is elusive, and we're left feeling empty.

Intrinsic motivation is the **internal drive and enjoyment** that you experience when you engage in activities for your inherent satisfaction and personal fulfillment.

Here's how emotional intelligence and intrinsic motivation work together:

- You are better able to identify activities that align with your interests, values, and personal goals. You tend to choose activities that genuinely resonate with you, which

increases your intrinsic motivation to engage in those activities.
- With a deep understanding of your own emotions, you know better how to motivate yourself and sustain motivation and passion over time—and how to motivate others to be their best selves.
- When you have confidence in your abilities, you are more likely to feel intrinsically motivated to set challenging yet attainable goals, to take on those challenges, and to persist in all your endeavors.
- You are better able to stay focused, persistent, and optimistic in facing any obstacles because you have a clear picture of who you are, what you're able to handle, and the goals in front of you that are going to bring you fulfillment and satisfaction in the doing.

#3 COLLABORATION IN RELATIONSHIPS

Relationships inevitably will involve differences of opinion and conflicts. Collaboration requires navigating challenges, disagreements, and high-pressure situations.

Here's how emotional intelligence influences collaboration:

- You understand others' perspectives, as well as your own emotions, so you can approach conflicts with empathy, active listening, and a focus on finding common ground. You are better able to prevent conflicts from escalating.
- You stay composed and focused during collaborative efforts. You are more likely to recognize and address any

biases or limitations you might have, which helps you forge a more objective and unbiased collaboration. This increases the chances for more productive outcomes and finding mutually beneficial solutions.
- The capacity to regulate and manage your own emotions helps you effectively foster a cooperative environment, create the space for collaborative problem-solving, and maintain positive relationships.

These three ingredients fuel your energy and spark your passion for everything you do.

They enhance your professional and personal relationships by promoting compassion, effective communication, self-awareness, and emotional regulation—skills all relationships need!

In the workplace, these qualities facilitate trust and understanding among team members, leading to more successful collaborative endeavors. Developing and honing emotional intelligence skills can significantly improve an individual's ability to collaborate and achieve collective goals.

Another way these ingredients beautifully cross-reference is in growing meaningful and positive relationships in terms of support, encouragement, and inspiration. When people feel a sense of belonging and positive social reinforcement, their motivation is boosted to engage in activities that align with their values and interests.

Here's a bring-it-down-to-earth illustration of how all this applies to your everyday life:

Sarah, a dedicated professional, is at odds with her colleague, Pete, who consistently takes credit for her ideas at work. It just happened again in a team meeting with the boss. Anger and frustration well up—she can feel it in her body—prompting her to consider her response to Pete.

At this moment, Sarah's imagination is engaged. She envisions two paths before her: one steeped in resentment and the desire for revenge, and the other illuminated by understanding and compassion. She senses the emotional weight of these choices through awareness of the heaviness of anger and the lightness of forgiveness in her body.

Sarah is reminded of her passion for her work and remembers that Pete has shared those feelings. She stops to listen to her inner voice; it helps her see how this negative energy is sapping passion, not only for her, but also for him. It points out that escalating the situation with anger won't get her anywhere. She feels the urge to choose the path of compassion toward another. At that moment, Sarah recognizes that Pete's behavior may stem from insecurity rather than malice. With this insight, she resolves the issue with kindness and open communication, relaying passion and showing compassion in her response.

Looking through the Emotional Lens with the help of these three gifts allows you to navigate the complexities of your intentions and foster a more authentic and peaceful way of living.

PAYOFF: PASSIONATE PURSUIT

Now that you know all of this valuable stuff, it's time to discover—or dust off—your passion so you can **explore the things you are particularly passionate about.**

Finding one's passion is an individual journey that will vary from person to person. Here are two activities I like as a prompt for your process to discover your passionate pursuits:

1. Reflect on your interests, values, strengths, and aspirations through whatever practice you prefer. Ask yourself thought-provoking questions like:

> "What activities make me lose track of time?"
> "What topics or causes am I most passionate about?"

This process of self-reflection can help you identify areas that genuinely resonate with you.

2. Actively explore different activities, hobbies, and subjects that spark your imagination. Be open to trying new things and stepping out of your comfort zone. Attend workshops, take courses, and join clubs or communities related to various interests. Engaging in diverse experiences allows you to gain exposure to different domains. It helps you uncover new interests and passions you might never have considered.

Curiosity often leads to passion, which indicates genuine enthusiasm and a desire to learn more about a particular area. Pay attention to the activities or topics that naturally pique your attention and ignite your curiosity. Follow those threads and delve deeper. Read books, watch documentaries, listen to podcasts, or engage in conversations around those subjects.

Remember, passions can evolve and change over time, so it's essential to stay open and flexible in your exploration along your Whole Person path.

MUCH MORE THAN GIVING BACK

For me, coaching youth athletics was a natural fit because of my experience as an athlete and the huge lessons I learned from my coaches over the years. Coaching youth sports can bring about a range of personal benefits.

A big one for me is the opportunity to make a meaningful and positive impact on the lives of young athletes. As a coach, I have the chance to instill values like teamwork, discipline, perseverance, and sportsmanship. By helping these kids develop their skills and confidence, I'm able to contribute to their personal growth and development, both on and off the field.

I serve as a mentor and role model for these kids, offering guidance, support, and encouragement. I've also built many strong connections with their families and fellow coaches. These incredibly rewarding relationships bring me a sense of fulfillment and camaraderie.

Effective coaching requires clear and concise communication, both with individuals and the team as a whole. I learned to adapt my communication style with different athletes and effectively convey instructions, give (and take) feedback, and kindle their motivation. These skills have proved to be transferable in all other areas of my life, personally and professionally.

Coaching also challenges you to be patient, empathetic, and understanding, which feeds personal qualities like compassion and resilience. I hope I have met those challenges.

Challenged and changed

At one of our practices, a fight broke out between two of my players. My first instinct was to grab them both by the shirt sleeves and severely discipline them. Instead, I asked them to separate and take five (Truth? I was buying time to figure out what to do next!). I took that pause to center myself while each of them stood in their place, shuffling their feet back and forth and huffing and puffing with barely repressed anger.

I approached Alex, one of our most gifted and talented players and a natural leader. I started asking questions about what happened while hopefully suppressing any accusatory tone. As it turned out, Alex was frustrated about the other player's effort during practice.

I understood and empathized with the young player. I complimented him on being a natural leader with strong drive and good practice skills. He nodded and seemed to respond well. By then, they both had cooled down, and I made a request of Alex: "Everyone on this team looks up to you, and I'm not saying that you have to apologize. But it's important to the team that you walk over there and make things right."

That's all it took. He trusted me, and I could tell he knew what to do. He walked over; they talked for a few seconds and shook hands.

I'll always remember that experience because my initial response was to throttle them both! Still, the way I was able to handle the situation made us all the better for it. I know the team learned something that day, and so did I.

Witnessing the growth and progress of young athletes under my guidance has left a lasting and meaningful impression on me. My original intention was to give back to the community by coaching. What happened is that I got more out of it than I could possibly have put in.

HERE'S THE (INTER)CONNECTION

Three tips have helped me expand my Emotional Lens:

1) Practice Mindfulness: Mindfulness meditation has helped me become more attuned to my inner ecosystem, which enhances all three gifts: imagination, inner voice, and sensation of the six senses. Regular practice allows me to observe my thoughts without judgment and become more in touch with my intuition.

2) Trust Your Gut: I've practiced focusing on my "gut feelings," or my instincts. These subtle sensations often signal that your inner voice is trying to communicate with you. Practice trusting your instincts when you are in the process of making a decision. Start with smaller, simpler decisions and grow from there.

3) Be Patient: Developing my inner voice has taken time and practice. Being patient with myself does not come naturally to me! I choose to trust that it will become more apparent as I continue to work on it.

WRAPPIN' IT UP

Circling back to the beginning of this chapter, our Emotional Lens influences how our internal narrative sees our world. You can see that it has a giant role to play in creating our reality—specifically, the reality we *want* to live in.

Imagination, inner voice, and sensation of the six senses are interconnected aspects of our cognitive and sensory processes that can shape our emotional experiences. They contribute to perceiving and interpreting events, generating emotional responses, and regulating emotions.

Pursuing passion is a pivotal component of the Whole Person Paradigm journey. This path invites us on a transformative ride through the intricate landscape of our emotions, with the help of our Emotional Lens. Take a moment to be still, open up your lens, and take in the following:

> **Imagine for a moment a serene garden.** In this garden, emotions bloom like vibrant flowers, each with a distinct color and fragrance. As we step into this lush realm, your sensation of the six senses awakens. You can feel the softness of petals beneath your fingers, the gentle sway of the breeze, and warm sunlight caressing your skin. You invite in and deeply experience your feelings, to touch and be touched by them.
>
> Your inner voice accompanies you through this garden of emotions. It whispers insights on the

breeze, offering guidance on how to navigate the complex interplay of desires and intentions. This voice is not one of judgment but reflection, inviting you to pause and consider the motives underlying your actions.

As you continue to stroll, your imagination, so stirred by the beauty around you, comes alive by the feelings that have touched you and the gentle prodding of your inner voice. It sparks new ways to think about your goals, plans, and relationships, helping you to visualize them with curiosity, joy, excitement, and creativity. Bask in these musings, noticing what particular thing—a goal, for example—grabs your attention. Give it space to bloom for a few moments.

And, as I stated at the beginning of this chapter, I'll wrap up with the most important thing: **The highest expression of the Emotional Lens is unconditional love.** Wow! That's a worthwhile aspirational invitation, right?

We talked about expanding the possibility of unconditional love through the Spiritual Lens. Now, we're practicing with our gifts and harnessing our passion to explore our *expression* of love. I'm not here to define love, but I think we can all agree that it's something good, so start your exploration there, just knowing (and NOT knowing) its goodness.

Contemplate and practice how you can experience more of it in different ways. It starts with learning how to love yourself and take care of yourself, and then, as regards others. As the saying goes, put on your own oxygen mask before helping your fellow passengers with theirs.

GOING DEEPER

Feel free to jot down anything that comes up for you. Homework: Walk through this garden a few more times and take more notes. Write a personal peace and prosperity mission statement for yourself.

NOTES

INNERCHAPTER
YOUR DASH
(Whaddaya gonna do wit it?)

THE DASH BY LINDA ELLIS

I read of a man who stood to speak at the funeral of a friend.
He referred to the dates on the tombstone from the beginning to the end.

He noted first came the date of birth and spoke of the following date with tears.
But he said what mattered most of all was the dash between those years.

For that dash represents all the time that they spent life on Earth.
And now only those who loved them know what that little line is worth.

For it matters not how much we own, the cars, the house, the cash.
What matters is how we live and love, and how we spend our dash.

So, think about this long and hard. Are there things you'd like to change?

For you never know how much time is left that still can be rearranged.

If we could just slow down enough to consider what's true and real,
And always try to understand the way other people feel.

And be less quick to anger, and show appreciation more,
and love the people in our lives like we've never loved before.

If we treat each other with respect and more often wear a smile,
remembering that this special dash might only last a little while.

So, when your eulogy is being read with your life's actions to rehash,
would you be proud of the things they say about how you spent your dash?

CHAPTER THREE

MENTAL LENS— PRONUNCIATION
Speak your world into existence

You are energy plus information within space and time. You have a brain to think, emotions to feel, *and a mouth to speak*—all of which create your existence and your relationship to everyone and everything else in existence.

The Spiritual Lens and Emotional Lens are containers for the Mental Lens. **The spiritual is the space; the emotional is what's driving you. The mental introduces choice**—making a choice, not making a choice, choosing from a place of consciousness, or in determinist terms, giving yourself over to external circumstances with a knee-jerk reaction.

Whatever that choice may be, **you choose to speak your world into existence.**

Examining your Mental Lens is a profound journey on the Whole Person Paradigm path. You will delve into the realm of your thoughts, words and expressions which, in combination, have the potential to be powerful forces for positive change and understanding, not to mention your own freedom and happiness.

> Watch your thoughts; they become words.
> Watch your words; they become actions.
> Watch your actions; they become habits.
> Watch your habits; they become character.
> Watch your character, for it becomes your destiny.
>
> —*This version is commonly attributed to Ralph Waldo Emerson and seen on a wall in my client's reception lobby*

EXPAND AND DEVELOP YOUR MENTAL LENS

The edges of the Mental Lens in the THPM are *self-awareness*, *imagination*, and *choice*.

Picture this: You are in a vast mental landscape, a canvas upon which thoughts and words paint the tapestry of your interactions. Self-awareness is your first brushstroke. It allows you to observe your thoughts and recognize the power they hold. With this awareness, you gain the ability to pause, reflect, imagine, and choose the colors you wish to add to the canvas of your expression.

> "It is something to be able to paint a particular picture or to carve a statue, and so to make a few objects beautiful, but it is far more glorious to carve and paint the very atmosphere and medium through which we look, which morally we can do."
>
> —Henry David Thoreau

Isn't that a great description of your Mental Lens?

How does it play out (and interplay) in our lives?

> **John's wife, Natasha, shares an idea** with him. John disagrees strongly with the idea. In this moment, self-awareness dawns on him as he recognizes the choices before him. John can either respond with harsh criticism and dismissiveness and darken the canvas with negativity or employ his imagination and choose words that encourage constructive dialogue. And avoid potential bodily harm...

Imagination is the second brushstroke, allowing us to see beyond the surface of our interactions. It invites us to envision the impact of our words on others and consider the emotions they may be having. We can shape our expressions with imagination to bridge gaps, foster empathy, and build connections.

> Drawing from his imaginative capacity, John can see what is triggering him to want to respond negatively, and he can also picture how Natasha might be feeling. He begins to think about the idea more clearly and creatively, which calms his triggered emotions.

Choice is the hand that guides the brush and determines the strokes. We have the power to choose our words consciously and select those that align with our values and intentions while creating communication that is meaningful to our listener.

This gift of choice distinguishes us as beings capable of transformation and growth. We are empowered to communicate with authenticity, empathy, and the intention to uplift ourselves and others in the shared tapestry of human connection.

> Clearly seeing the choices before him now, John chooses to frame his response by acknowledging Natasha's perspective and suggesting an alternative viewpoint. His tone is positive and nonjudgmental. Natasha hears him; John has maintained harmony in their conversation and a spirit of collaboration and mutual respect. They go on to discuss the idea, pros and cons, and their collective imagination ultimately creates a great result.

YOU ARE NOT YOUR STORY

Self-awareness. This gift involves deeply understanding oneself, including thoughts, emotions, strengths, weaknesses, and communication style. You have the ability to monitor and understand those thoughts, emotions and behaviors. You develop the ability to recognize in real time how your words and actions are affecting others—and identify and manage biases, assumptions, or ineffective communication patterns.

You are able to adapt your speech to different contexts, situations, and audiences and respond appropriately. Through self-awareness, you can actively listen, seek feedback, and continuously improve your communication skills.

In general, **self-aware people are able to communicate with more empathy, more respect, and more inclusion, which leads to much more effective and meaningful interactions.**

Bonnie Artman Fox, a guest on my *Tao of Pizza* podcast, shared Tasha Eurich's study findings, which reveal that most people think they are self-aware, but only 10-15% have achieved that status. "Having self-awareness," says Eurich, an organizational psychologist and researcher, "means fully knowing who you are—your values, passions, goals, personality, strengths and weaknesses—and understanding how others perceive you." (You can read more about Tasha Eurich's research in her book *Insight: Why We're Not as Self-Aware as We Think, and How Seeing Ourselves Clearly Helps Us Succeed at Work and in Life.*)

Bonnie has also shared her insights on a fascinating aspect of self-awareness, or lack thereof. She is an Executive Coach and Accredited Boss Whisperer® who works with "abrasive leaders", defined by the Boss Whispering Institute as "leaders who rub their co-workers the wrong way. Their words and actions create interpersonal friction that... can erode employee motivations and organizational productivity." (Know anyone like this?)

One of the most profound things about her work is seeing that most abrasive leaders are completely unaware of the negative effect their behavior is having on others! The good news is that this means they are coachable, and Bonnie has seen great success in turning around an abrasive leadership style.

Two powerful examples of our human tendency to ignore the dusty spots clouding our self-awareness mirror!

Self-awareness affirmations:

1. I am able to stand apart from my thoughts and feelings and examine or change them.
2. I am aware of the way I think about things and how it impacts my attitudes and behaviors and the results I'm getting in my life.
3. I am aware of a difference between my biological, genealogical, psychological, and sociological scripting—and my own deep inner presence.
4. When someone's response to what I say or do challenges the way I see myself, I am able to evaluate the feedback against deep personal self-knowledge and learn from it.

Imagination. This is how we paint that mental landscape—come up with the atmosphere and the medium, as Thoreau suggests. ***Our imagination is what is most unique in us, as we***

are creative in our thinking, worldview, and how we act and communicate with others. Open yourself to creative suggestions whenever and wherever you can.

Imagination affirmations:

1. I think ahead.
2. I visualize my life beyond its present reality.
3. I use visualization to help reaffirm and realize my goals.
4. I look for new and creative ways to solve problems in a variety of situations and value the different views of others.

Choice. The choices we make have a profound effect on our mindset. Recognizing that we have agency and the power to make choices gives us a sense of control, ownership, and personal responsibility. Conscious decision-making enables us to align our actions with our goals and values, which can positively influence our mindset.

Embracing the ability to make choices, even in challenging situations, cultivates a belief in our capacity to learn, adapt, and improve. This is why it is good not to shy away from making a choice—you benefit whether it turns out to be a "great" choice or a "poor" choice!

Your choices regarding what you say and how you say it directly influence your speech—literally speaking your world (reality) into existence! The ability to make conscious choices about your words, tone, and delivery can impact the effectiveness and impact of your communication. Thoughtful choices in speech can also contribute to building rapport, resolving conflicts, and conveying your ideas effectively and with impact.

If you've ever spent an hour writing a two-paragraph email to a client, employee, or auntie, you know what I'm talking about!

Choice affirmations:

1. I choose to make and keep promises to myself and others.
2. I act on my inner imperatives, even when it means swimming upstream.
3. I consistently develop the ability to set and achieve meaningful goals in my life.
4. I subordinate my moods to my commitments when necessary.

With relaxed and developed self-awareness, you know clearly what you want to say and what emotions or thoughts might be inhibiting you from saying it. You are able to tailor your speech to be more persuasive, engaging, and empathetic. You can choose to call up your imagination as you create and deliver your message to a particular audience.

It's important to note that the interplay among these gifts will vary A LOT from person to person. Each individual's experiences, beliefs, and practices will influence how their human gifts will impact their mindset and, in turn, how they relate to the people around them. **The beauty is that we each have our own unique expression of the world to share and exchange.**

TELL A MORE OPTIMISTIC YET REALISTIC STORY

Even though you are NOT your story, you have a story as part of the reality you create. Cultivating body-mind awareness and making empowering choices go a long way to helping you develop a more positive, compassionate, and growth-oriented mindset—and a more optimistic, yet realistic story that you tell yourself and express into the world. And your imagination makes it unique, fun, and exciting! Allow yourself to pay attention to this practice, always being gentle and self-forgiving. Such as...

> **Headline: Backyard Buddha Becomes Bully!** It all started in the serene setting of my backyard. Under the guidance of a wise meditation teacher, I set myself on a journey to practice the art of Metta Meditation, a type of Buddhist meditation to cultivate kindness for all beings (including oneself). It's also known as a lovingkindness meditation. For a few weeks, I delved into the depths of my mind several times a day.
>
> The process began with closing my eyes and focusing on my breath. As I breathed in and out, I imagined a world where all beings were in peace and harmony. This visualization challenged my self-awareness as I had to extend empathy even to my perceived enemies, to wish them well and hope for their happiness.

The power of imagination played a pivotal role as I envisioned this universal serenity, picturing people of all backgrounds and walks of life coexisting in perfect peace. It was a profound experience, connecting me to a wellspring of compassion within myself that I had never fully tapped into.

My inner voice guided me through the meditation, gently reminding me to release grudges or resentments. It encouraged me to make the choice to let go of negativity and embrace empathy instead. The intention was mine, and as I made it, I felt a weight lifting from my heart.

As the meditation session neared its end, my consciousness soared to new heights. I felt a sense of tranquility and interconnectedness with all living beings. It was a state of bliss and enlightenment I had never experienced before in my life.

As I emerged from this elevated state and opened my eyes, the first thing I saw was a huge wasp buzzing dangerously close to me. With lightning precision born from my newfound inner peace, I dealt the wasp a swift, decisive, and deadly flick of my finger and thumb, killing it instantly.

The irony and humor were not lost on me—I had to chuckle at this unexpected turn of events. The same elevated state of consciousness that had led to empathy for enemies had also granted me the ability to dispatch a common wasp with surprising skill.

I realized that life could still surprise us with its little quirks, even in the pursuit of inner peace. The journey of self-discovery and enlightenment is full of delightful contradictions. Be ready for it!

CHOOSE TO COMMUNICATE CLEARLY WITH CONFIDENCE AND CLAIRVOYANCE

Through our Mental Lens, we develop the inner dialog—self-talk—that represents who we are to ourselves. When we turn that expression outward, it becomes communication. So, again, it is self first, then outward (like the oxygen mask). Inside-Out.

Speech is something that most of us take for granted, like walking and breathing. *It most definitely is more than that!* Speech plays a pivotal role in unlocking human potential in these three major ways:

Shaping beliefs and mindset. The words we use in our speech, both internally and externally, shape our beliefs and mindset, just as our beliefs and mindset influence our words. It's an interplay that can either go positively or down the negative rabbit hole. When we practice positive self-talk, affirmations, and empowering language, we cultivate a growth mindset, boost self-confidence, and enhance resilience.

Conversely, negative or self-limiting speech can reinforce self-doubt and limit our potential. And make us mean knuckleheads!

By being mindful of your language and consciously choosing empowering and growth-oriented words, you can literally transform your beliefs and mindset, which will lead to more extraordinary achievements and personal development. A moment ago, I mentioned the term "practice."

Here's a glimpse of mine ...

One powerful shift I learned from Wendy Palmer was to say *yes, and...* instead of *yeah, but...* What's the difference? *Yeah, but...* is conflict waiting to happen! A sincere *yes, and...* invokes respect and shared values. It adds to, rather than cuts off, compassionate communication.

In my twenties, I learned to transform problems into challenges by naming them accordingly. "Challenges" became "opportunities." There are many words I have replaced in my vocabulary, and it's something I'm constantly evolving. I also do this with my kids and with my team.

Our company recently upgraded our order processing systems, and the manager responsible for the project suggested we call it a "speed bump." Well, I don't want any speed bumps in our order processing systems! After a short conversation, we decided to call it "customs" because it reminded us of the excitement of world travel, and the main reason we needed to upgrade our systems was that all of our orders were custom. Get it?

Self-awareness, imagination, and choice, right there!

> "Finding your voice is Effectiveness, and helping others find their voice is Greatness."
>
> —Steven Covey

Inspiring and motivating others. Stephen Covey's quote comes from his book, *The 8th Habit: From Effectiveness to Greatness*. Our voice, expressed in our speech, can inspire, motivate, and influence others. By sharing stories, experiences, and aspirations, we can influence and motivate those around us to reach their full potential. Encouraging and uplifting words can instill confidence, ignite passion, and drive individuals to pursue their goals and dreams. Through motivational speeches, mentoring, coaching, or even everyday conversations, people positively impact others and contribute to their growth and development every single day.

Indeed, using words that convey collaboration and positivity can greatly influence others. Here are nine examples:

1. Instead of "contract," use "agreement."
2. Instead of "sign here," use "approve here."
3. Instead of "demand," use "request."
4. Instead of "criticize," use "constructive feedback."
5. Instead of "complain," use "express concerns."
6. Instead of "failure," use "learning experience" or "growth opportunity."
7. Instead of "blame," use "share responsibility."

8. Instead of "obey," use "cooperate" or "collaborate."
9. Instead of "hierarchy," use "team structure" or "network of support."

Building relationships and establishing connections. Speech is crucial to building relationships and establishing connections with others. It can open up opportunities for collaboration, learning and innovation. Meaningful conversations, active listening, and empathetic responses lead to understanding and cooperation.

These interpersonal connections provide support networks, opportunities for mentorship, and the exchange of knowledge and experiences. *Through the Mental Lens, you develop and refine various skills that are essential for professional growth, such as public speaking, presentations, negotiation, and persuasion.* Mastering these skills boosts your confidence, influence and ability to, in turn, inspire and motivate others to expand their potential.

WHAT'S IN A WORD?

> "Words are, in my not-so-humble opinion, our most inexhaustible source of magic. Capable of both inflicting injury, and remedying it."
>
> —*Albus Dumbledore (J. K. Rowling)*

When we speak our world into existence, the words we choose impact our environment in powerful ways. Words and language have been built into societies for 100,000 years (give or take). In today's society, history is happening so fast that it can be a challenge to catch up with the concepts and ideas that are evolving and being expressed through words. They can have hidden meanings, historical contexts, and connotations we aren't even aware of.

Often, we can choose words that are offensive to others without knowing why. "To grandfather in," for example, was a term of Black voter suppression during the Reconstruction period. Many people use it today, innocent of its history (including me until I was informed of its history by my editor).

One aspect of cultivating self-awareness is to be mindful of the meaning of the words we choose to the best of our ability, and to uncover those vocabulary biases. Then, we can use our imagination to generate different words or phrases to convey the same meaning.

It's a kind of innovation to use language that creates environments that are more open to collaboration and cooperation. In the example I just gave about good ol' Grandpa, something like "retroactively accepted as up to code" conveys the same meaning more accurately without involving a vague and potentially harmful metaphor. Sounds a little more official, too.

Having said this (and maybe anticipating your pushback?), choosing language that affirms life is a tricky business. I don't want to be judged for words I choose without knowing their hidden meanings, and I don't want to be nitpicked—that's probably another one :-)—for every minor possible offense. I DO want to be careful and intentional with my words. **When we choose our speech with cultivated self-awareness, we can imagine better ways to collaborate, cooperate, and elevate the human condition, at least to the best of our ability.**

We also have the choice not to judge ourselves too harshly or judge others for their lack of awareness and sensitivity to these things. Grace and nonjudgmental attitudes are much more effective than cancel culture. Remember, relationships matter most. We're in this together.

THE PAYOFF: SIX PRACTICES OF CONSCIOUS ACCOUNTABILITY

1. You are your word. Another aspect of how we communicate and interact with each other is commitment. If I make a commitment to someone, I'm going to "keep my word" because I honestly think it's the right thing to do. And I've found that when you always keep your word, things just get easier for you.

People know they can count on you. There's less friction and more trust, more intimacy and better relationships. From the Spiritual Lens, you want to show up for what you mentally want to commit to. Sometimes, that means showing up when you *need* to, whether or not you *want* to. It takes some discernment to practice this in your daily life because you can get busy, things can get complicated, and plans change. *But you gave your word. Ultimately, of course, it's your choice to keep it or not.*

Years ago, a speaker at an Amway meeting I attended said something I've never forgotten: "Do what you need to do when you need to do it, whether you want to or not." This is something I try to live by because I believe none of it is worth anything unless we're showing up in people's lives, for our community, and for our friends and family.

These are my rules of thumb for being true to my word:

- Say what you want; say what you're going to do.
- Do what you say you're going to do.
- Be cautious about making commitments, and dedicate yourself to keeping them.
- Correct course when you can't keep a commitment (because, after all, shit can happen).

In our company, we have three levels of commitment to execute on our word. Level one is for emergencies—things that are urgent and extra important need to be dealt with within fifteen minutes. Level two is for things like returning a phone call or providing an update, and must be completed within two hours. The last level involves things like proposals, gathering information, and other longer-term commitments that need to be at least addressed, if not completed, within twenty-four hours.

It is a work in progress for all of us; we're not striving for perfection, and these commitments can involve several course corrections. However, they serve to honor everyone's time and to avoid the expectation that businesses can have of demanding that twenty-four-hour stuff get done in fifteen minutes, no matter what. More importantly, having this clear commitment to each other strengthens our relationships and helps clarify expectations.

2. Don't BS yourself—it's a trap. "Know thyself" doesn't mean memorizing your track record or resume. That's all autobiographical and egotistical, and if you allow it to become your identity, you will be able to talk yourself into just about anything, learn nothing—and it will bring you down, no joke.

Knowing who you are is a continuous and never-ending process of discovery along the Whole Person Paradigm path. It starts with holding yourself accountable TO yourself by telling yourself the truth.

3. Make your word count. When you speak, you are delivering a message that's important to you, so make sure it will be heard. Create clarity, open up engagement, and nail it! Notice how it landed, and exchange feedback. Claim the feedback and try again. You will connect more closely to others, put people in a position to succeed, elevate and distinguish yourself, and generate excellence everywhere you turn.

4. Don't criticize, condemn, complain, or—God forbid—gossip. There's an interesting relationship between criticizing others and criticizing ourselves. The mind-as-mirror metaphor reinforces that outward criticism is mirrored by self-criticism, only human nature makes us much more critical of ourselves.

> **In one of his *Awakening Leadership* program talks** I attended, I recall how John Mackey, the founder of Whole Foods Market, reframed the

idea of complaints: He used the complaints they received as catalysts for personal and organizational transformation. From my notes: *Every time I had a breakthrough, Whole Foods had a breakthrough. Every time I was ready to have my next breakthrough, Whole Foods would show me the way through what people were complaining about.*

Each time he identified something wrong within the company, Mackey chose to seek innovative solutions, which led to breakthroughs for him and the company. His approach to addressing complaints was to foster growth and improvement, generated by his belief in actively seeking solutions rather than just complaining about the problems. The potential complaints he identified became an opportunity for positive change, emphasizing the importance of taking action to address concerns and drive transformation.

Isn't this a great take on complaining? **Complaint is a window into an opportunity for transformation or breakthrough.** If you hear yourself complaining, use it to create transformative opportunities.

During a meeting with our strategic partners, my boss attempted to impress them by stating we practiced "duplicity," thinking it was a strategic term. The room fell silent in confusion, and he looked perplexed. I felt embarrassed for him in that moment because I understood the reason for the confusion. Later, I privately explained to him Steven Covey's use of the principle of *avoiding* "duplicity"—saying one thing while doing another, which is usually followed by gossip. It was awkward because here I was in my twenties, and he was in his fifties, and I was calling him out. But I did not mean to criticize him at all. I respectfully highlighted the misunderstanding; he didn't push back, we diffused an awkward situation, and he learned something new to consider for future communications.

5. "Be 'hearty in your approbation and lavish in your praise,' and people will cherish your words and treasure them and repeat them over a lifetime—repeat them years after you have forgotten them." Dale Carnegie nails it again. It doesn't cost us anything to be kind, so why don't we do more of it?

6. Speak gratitude. "Rejoice always" (1 Thessalonians 5:16-17) is one of the shortest verses in the Bible, and it is radiant with heavenly Light. As humans, we share the ability to choose joy from moment to moment in our lives. As our mind tends to go down an unpleasant path, we can stop it in its tracks by following this amazing command.

A gratitude practice can be an excellent way to remind yourself to rejoice. You can find research everywhere that confirms the efficacy of gratitude practice for outlook, moods, physical health, and so on. My practice takes just a few minutes every other day or so.

It's essential to be specific. Find the little things to be grateful for—if it seems mundane, IT'S NOT. Be grateful for your body, for water, for the fact that you can move, for the cappuccino you just had, for sex, and for the soft sheets on your bed. Write a quick list of what you "get" to do—*especially the things you don't want to do:* meet with the accountant, take out the garbage, do the dishes, give or get bad news...

Focusing on joyful thoughts will light up both your mind and your heart, enabling you to find more pleasure in your life. Choosing joy will influence and strengthen those around you. It develops your network of supportive relationships. **It's the best self-fulfilling prophecy you can imagine!**

HERE'S THE (INTER)CONNECTION

By integrating our human gifts of self-awareness, imagination and choice, we create the internal reality that we speak out into the world to connect with and impact others. Choosing positive self-talk boosts confidence and clarity and continually feeds on itself like a magnificent buffet. We create a self-fulfilling prophecy for our own growth.

> **One of my mentors is a seriously talented electrician.** He is a master controls programmer and a gifted plan reader. He has executed complex projects like water treatment plants, nuclear power plants, and sophisticated conveyor systems. He's famous for telling one of his journeymen, "I don't have time to explain the theory. Just do it the way I said."

I love a story he once told me, especially because he's so accomplished that I could never imagine him being anything other than supremely confident. Not so! When he started to train to be an electrician, he was really nervous—the task seemed daunting. So, he made a practice of telling himself daily, "I'm an electrician. I'm an awesome electrician." He repeated the mantra until it actually came true. That self-talk drove him to show up every day with confidence, make great choices, learn expertise, and excel to the top of this field.

WRAPPIN' IT UP

To close, I want to repeat Ralph Waldo Emerson's quote from the beginning of this chapter because it says it all:

> *Watch your thoughts; they become words.*
> *Watch your words; they become actions.*
> *Watch your actions; they become habits.*
> *Watch your habits; they become character.*
> *Watch your character, for it becomes your destiny.*

GOING DEEPER

Remember the kick-ass tetrahedron Whole Person model-building practice you did a few chapters back (that might now be your most favorite desk ornament)? Time to pick it up again—or, if you CHOSE to skip it, now is a good time to CHOOSE to do it!

The reason? Holding the tetrahedron in your hands and experiencing the interrelationships is more powerful than just reading about it. The brain loves the six senses to be activated—it's called active learning, which enhances the brain's synaptic plasticity.

Now for some contemplation: Look through each of the three lenses we've covered so far. Notice the shared edges, aka human gifts. Notice how Mental self-awareness is different from Spiritual self-awareness, although they are connected.

Think about recognizing the lenses as an effective way to understand who you are and to offer new perspectives on how to view the world. What area of your life could be enhanced by looking at it through your Spiritual, Mental, and Emotional Lens?

Before you jump into the Action lens, check out the Innerchapter that follows. It will shed some light on how language generates a representation of reality that, although useful, is not the same as the direct experience of reality. Have some fun with it!

NOTES

INNERCHAPTER
THE ZEN OF LANGUAGE
(Words are tricky because worldviews are sticky)

The story of how Hui-Yu became the Sixth Patriarch of Zen Buddhism is a legendary and deeply significant tale within the Zen tradition that has lessons for us today. Many versions have evolved over the centuries, and what follows is a little Asian philosophy and a little Hiddle-Haddle. What's key here is the poems and rich interpretations that can expand our self-awareness.

Hui-Yu was born into a poor family, and his father died when he was very young, so Hui-Yu had to support his family by gathering and selling firewood. Even without any education or literacy, he had a natural and deep understanding of the Dharma (Buddhist teachings). As a young man, Hui-Yu had an awakening and traveled many miles to study with the Fifth Patriarch, Hung-Jen, in the East Mountain monastery.

The Fifth Patriarch recognized Hui-Yu's spiritual potential but, because of his lowly background, assigned him to hard labor rather than allowing him to participate in the regular monastic activities.

One day, the elderly Hung-Jen announced that he would pass the patriarch on to the monk who could best demonstrate his understanding of the nature of enlightenment. The head monk, Hau-Tu, who was considered the most likely successor, composed a verse and inscribed it on the wall of the monastery:

> "The enlightened body is the Bodhi tree,
> The mind is like a clear mirror standing.
> At all times, we must strive to polish it,
> And must not let dust collect."

When Hui-Yu heard the monk's verse, he composed his own in response and asked someone to inscribe it on the wall since he was illiterate:

> "The Bodhi is not a tree,
> There is no clear mirror standing.
> Not one thing exists,
> What is there for dust to cling to?"

When the Fifth Patriarch read these two profound yet simple poems, he recognized that the humble, uneducated Hui-Yu was more enlightened than his best student. Consequently, he made Hui-Yu the Sixth Patriarch, entrusting the line of succession to him.

The "best and brightest" disciple crafted a brilliant poem using nature as a metaphor—Bodhi as tree, mind as mirror, and making sure to let no dust cling to the mirror is a fantastic concept.

The dust might represent the different worldviews, paradigms or ways of being that we inherit—and which will cloud our view of reality.

However, Hau-Tu's analysis, as seen through his Spiritual Lens, was limited to the "parts."

Hui-Yu's response to the concepts and clever metaphors in Hau-Tu's poem unveils that the Bodhi isn't even a tree, and there is no mirror; the human mind isn't mentioned. There is nothing to polish. There is nothing for dust to cling to—in fact, there is no dust!

The tree, the dust and the mirror are all just constructs. Hui-Yu was able to step back from these "earthly" elements and beyond the distinctions to see the "whole", to see with energy.

Hui Yu's poem goes beyond the reality of the human experience to the interconnectedness of all things and exposes the fallacy of human social constructs like tree/body/mind/mirror. He recognizes the inherent purity and emptiness of all things, including the mind. ***In reality, it is all jest :) one thing. Energy.***

So, how is this useful? Well, when we sift through all the constructs and the cloudiness, **we ARE energy.** The two Zen poems work together as a reflection on the nature of the self, our interconnectedness to each other, and to something beyond ourselves.

In Hau-Tu's verse, we can see where the body is like the Bodhi tree, and the mind is like a mirror. Letting no speck of dust cling to it is a concise yet profound reflection on self-awareness and the constant maintenance of one's spiritual clarity (as we have talked about in the last two chapters). You could build an amazing life around this first poem, embracing the practice of cleaning the dust from the thoughts and stories in your mind to keep your Lenses—your worldview—clean and pure.

I also like the comparison between the body and the Bodhi tree, a sacred fig tree under which the Buddha is said to have attained enlightenment. This suggests that the body serves as the vessel for our spiritual journey. Just as the Bodhi tree was the setting for the Buddha's awakening, our bodies are the canvas upon which we paint the story of our lives.

Self-awareness is the key to understanding the significance of this connection. We can navigate our journey with clarity and purpose by being acutely attuned to our thoughts, emotions, and physical sensations.

Having said all this, I'm not claiming to understand the meaning of both poems clearly! More than understanding them, they have invited me to embrace the mystery between what I know and what I know I don't know. This book provides some ways to practice uncovering the largest piece of the pie (from Chapter One), which is **"what I don't know that I don't know."** Be prepared... in Chapter Eight, we'll take these concepts to a whole other level!

CHAPTER FOUR

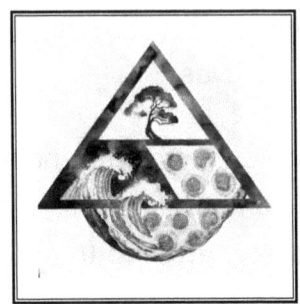

ACTION LENS—PRACTICE
Practice makes permanent (not always perfect)

Taking meaningful action is how we navigate life's intricate tapestry of choices and challenges on our way to the Whole Person Paradigm. The Action Lens is developing the behaviors that generate the experience of your Spiritual, Emotional, and Mental Lenses.

IT'S WALKY-WALKY, NOT TALKY-TALKY

When you're in a relationship, you can't talk yourself *out of* something that you behaved yourself *into*. My wife, Casey, will tell you that.

What does this mean? Well, I know all the right things to say to her. But when Monday morning rolls around and I'm jumping into full work mode, do I take that quick work phone call before I bring her coffee, or do I keep my head? Do I strategize in my mind about what I'm going to say in my next "big" business meeting, or do I actively listen to her explain for the seventh time how her father's coming to town and we're going to Top Golf?

These are the choices that circle in my head, which I suspect you can relate to in your own relationship(s)...

It may seem like I'm taking a shot at my wife, because I am. But let me explain. I signed up for the idea of serving my Worthy Queen like a Goddess. And I knew all along that Worthy Queen Goddesses can be a lot. And I'll leave it at that. But that is what I signed up for.

These inner tugs in two directions are not so much about communication itself; they're about the intentional behaviors (and perceived behaviors) that show I'm engaged with my Goddess in this relationship because it matters to her, and it matters to me. Our behaviors make a difference to each other.

The Action Lens is about speaking your world into existence AND making it a practice—within yourself, in your relationships, and out in the world—in a way that matters.

EXPAND AND DEVELOP YOUR ACTION LENS

We are delving deeper into the art of cultivating BEing by embracing your human gifts of *inner voice, sense of humor,* and *choice.* Practicing these gifts through the Action Lens empowers you to make wise and ethical decisions, forge a life of purpose, and navigate the myriad choices that will define your unique journey.

You know those people who love to be all "talky-talky" and forget about the walking their talk part? I'm sure you do! Here we are at "inside-out" again. It's fine to do the inner work with your other lenses (lifelong work, in fact), but it's just talky-talky if you do not craft and practice your script of a meaningful and virtuous life.

At some point, you gotta take it on the road.

P.S. My wife might also tell you that I am (and she is) still a work in progress. That's the path of the Whole Person Paradigm! Thank you, Goddess.

Let's break down the human gifts in the context of the Action Lens ...

Inner voice. Developing your inner voice enhances your decision-making, communication, and all-round well-being. Remember, your inner voice is that gut-feeling consciousness that knows the difference between social conditioning and natural principles. You can train your inner voice through positive self-talk to guide your responses to a situation; **the inner voice drives how you will speak and act.**

Here are eight things I do to help develop and nurture my inner voice:

1. Journaling. I keep a journal to record thoughts, feelings, experiences and ideas. Writing helps me clarify my inner voice and gain insights into my inner world. It's a practice that works best as a daily habit.

2. Asking myself questions. I often engage in self-inquiry by asking open-ended questions. For example: *What do I truly want in this situation?* Or, *What are my values and priorities in life?* A journal can be handy to take a stab at answering those questions.

3. Seeking solitude. Spending time alone helps me shut out distractions and dedicate time to connect with my inner self. I can listen to my thoughts and feelings without external influences.

4. Embracing creativity. I've engaged in creative activities such as coaching, fundraising, and writing. These activities help me tap into my subconscious mind and access my inner voice.

5. Practicing active listening. When I'm in conversation with others, I practice active listening (unfortunately, not every time) by trying to bring my full attention to them and tune into my inner voice's response to what is being said. My inner voice allows me to better understand what they are saying with more clarity and objectivity.

6. Following my passions. Thanks to my inner voice, I know the activities and interests that genuinely excite and inspire me, like getting a master's degree in Holistic Health, starting a business, and coaching youth athletics. The alignment of my inner voice and passion has led me to a more fulfilling life.

7. Reading—lots. I have this inexplicable gravitational pull towards non-fiction books. Even when I venture into the realm of fiction, my brain performs a systematic analysis that would make Sherlock Holmes proud. I'm always drawn to the underlying meaning of every seemingly insignificant idea. My inner voice feeds my reading comprehension and contemplation, and that exploration feeds my inner voice. It's a nice dance.

8. Seeking guidance. I've engaged with mentors, coaches, and friends who have guided and supported me in developing my inner voice (and much more…). Doing your homework transforms the coaching experience and unleashes your superpowers. Both in selecting the right guides AND doing the homework, including reporting back on what worked and what didn't.

9. Bonus: Have fun with 1 - 8!

> **One day, while enjoying lunch on the Napa River,** I cornered my friend and professional colleague, Rob, with a solemn expression that rivaled Shakespearean tragedy. "Rob," I sighed, "I simply don't have time to write in my journal anymore. But it's like my personal therapy, you know?"
>
> With a weary nod, Rob empathized, "I totally get it. Sometimes, I can't even find the time to eat breakfast. Life is chaos!"

Feeling reassured by his understanding, I continued, "Exactly! Lately, work, coaching, and the kids have me swamped."

Rob, now intrigued, asked, "How long does it usually take you to journal?"

With an air of utmost seriousness, I cleared my throat and replied, "Well, you see, Rob, it's an important task that takes approximately... seven minutes."

We both burst into laughter. "Seven minutes?" he laughed. "And you're complaining about that? That's less time than it takes me to find matching socks!"

We both chuckled at the absurdity of it all. It was the kind of laugh that made me realize that sometimes our excuses are the funniest things about us.

What seems hilarious to me about these practices is that most times, I have to give myself permission to engage in them—even though they're essential to me. Does that sound familiar to you? Life can be demanding, and the number and scope of what requires my attention seems to gather momentum daily. Even as I write this, I see that it's something I want to pay more attention to!

In any case, these practices have been essential to me, and maybe there are some that will become essential to you. The thing to remember is that **your inner voice is unique to you; others may manifest differently from you.** Developing it is a personal journey. The more you tune in and practice, the more in touch you will become with your inner wisdom and what you need and want.

Inner voice affirmation:

1. I sometimes feel an inner prompting that I should do something or that I shouldn't do something I'm about to do.
2. I sense the difference between "social conscience"—what society has conditioned me to value—and my own inner directives.
3. I inwardly sense the reality of universal principles such as integrity and trustworthiness.
4. I see a pattern in human experience—bigger than the society in which I live—that validates the reality of principles.

Sense of Humor. As you saw in Chapter One, the beauty of the human experience lies in our capacity for seriousness and our unique gift of humor. Humor serves as our playful companion on this journey. *It allows us to see life's complexities through a lighter lens, providing a momentary respite from the gravity of some of our choices.*

For me, humor is a friendly reminder that even the most challenging opportunities are not life's defining moments. This perspective relieves stress and helps me approach all of my endeavors with a more balanced and open heart (and with compassion for myself when I try too hard).

When those times of challenge come (perceived or real), engage your sense of humor—allow it to take over. Make it a game. My favorite cartoon show is *Wile E. Coyote and the Road Runner* because I find myself rooting for the bad guy; Wile E. Coyote always fails, and the Road Runner always gets away.

As I think about it, maybe you should look at opening this book like you would open up a box with an ACME (Artificially Intelligent Rocket Launcher) in it...and watch out!

Sense of Humor affirmations:

1. I can laugh at myself.
2. I don't struggle for perfection, and I realize that my mistakes are the only thing I can truly call my own.
3. I use humor to embrace my own humanness and share it with others.
4. I look for ways to turn lemons into lemonade through the creative force of humor and integrating learning experiences.

Choice. I've left choice for last because it's the most important one in terms of the Action Lens.

Imagine life as a grand stage where you are the playwright, director, and actor of your own story. The gift of choice allows you to craft the narrative, write the script, and act it out. You possess the extraordinary ability to determine your actions, mold your character, and impact the world in your unique way. ***Every decision, from the mundane to the profound, shapes the unfolding drama of your life.***

Consider a simple choice:

> **Marcus, a student, faces an upcoming exam.** He can choose to study diligently or procrastinate until the last minute. His inner voice serves as his guiding narrator. It whispers insights and wisdom, encouraging him to make choices that align with his long-term goals, such as dedicating focused time to study instead of succumbing to the "weapons of mass distraction" like social media or gaming.

A big part of choice is understanding the tradeoffs of your decisions. We make tradeoffs unconsciously in terms of our values. Marcus could be making a huge tradeoff if he ultimately chooses to procrastinate studying and is on the brink of failing his sophomore year!

Bringing this concept into your awareness unleashes the power of your choice. This is so important because when you make a choice to break your word, you hurt yourself, you might hurt others, and you damage trust (from others as well as trust in yourself). Trust is the gold standard for developing great relationships and expanding our capacity to give and receive love.

Choose to take action on the things that matter. **Ultimately, you get to choose to BE what you see as making a difference.**

Choice affirmations:

1. I am able to make and keep promises to myself and others.
2. I have the capacity to act on my inner imperatives, even when it means swimming upstream.
3. I have developed the ability to set and achieve meaningful goals in my life.
4. I can subordinate my moods to my commitments.

PROPER PRACTICE PREVENTS PISS POOR PERFORMANCE

We've been talking about "practice" a lot so far. Well, here's the secret about that: **Practice doesn't always make perfect. Practice makes permanent.** This is a crucial distinction because, as we have noticed, a lot of the habits we have "practiced" have not served our greater purpose. If you practice the wrong stuff, you are not developing something perfect for you. It will go permanently in the wrong direction or become messed up completely.

Bottom line? **Practice is a path to activating your individual and collective highest potential.** Holistic thinking and problem-solving involve widening your circle for compassion—and that takes practice. Getting to the ultimate source of your energy, vitality and wholeness—that takes practice. You don't get much more essential than that!

> "Our task must be to free ourselves from this prison by widening our circle of compassion to embrace all living creatures and the whole of nature in its beauty. Nobody is able to achieve this completely, but the striving for such achievement is in itself a part of the liberation and a foundation for inner security."
>
> —*Albert Einstein*

So, where do you start to practice what is meaningful and good and permanent?

You might have noticed that Einstein mentioned freeing ourselves from prison. The foundation of the Whole Person Paradigm is freedom from the prison that makes us feel separate from everything and everyone else. **Through practice, you can create portals that open to your particular expression of freedom.**

In practical terms, an aspect of your practice is going to be replacing or transcending habits, which we've been working with since Chapter One. So, the practice of freedom is to start noticing your thought habits, cravings, reactionary emotions and, most importantly, things that piss you off! *The things that piss you off are some of the most valuable resources you have to facilitate personal, professional and spiritual growth.*

Who knew?

When you notice and name it, you inform each choice—to keep it or set yourself free from it.

> "The gift of practice excels all gifts
> The experience of practice excels all experiences
> The joy of practice excels all joys."
>
> —The Buddha

Noticing and freeing yourself from the thoughts and habits that don't serve you are significant steps toward developing what is perfect for you. I might call it Spiritual Practice 101—even though it's a lifelong practice that you won't ever "graduate from" (and that's a good thing, as the gifts, experience and joys of practice will be with you forever).

MEDITATION—POSSIBLY THE BEST PRACTICE OF ALL

I've mentioned meditation a few times, and there's no time like the present to dig deeper!

Meditation is a way of showing up in your life from an unobstructed, clean, and spiritual place, outside the clutter inside your mind and the physical distractions around you.

There's no substitute for meditation, no class you can take to get the same result, no pill you can take. There's nothing like it and no other way around it. There are centuries of history and teachings about meditation techniques, some of which you've probably read or practice now. We won't go into all of them because meditation is a very personal and varied practice. I'll just share my experience and hope it helps you.

It took me a while to get to this place, but I now see meditation as a reward. It's like a mini-vacation, and I look forward to it. At some point, I shifted my attitude about meditation from an imperative that I *had* to do to **an attitude of gratitude, seeing it as a dance rather than a push through the mud.**

I have stopped asking, "Am I doing it right?"

I meditate almost every day, not for long periods of time. It's part of my day, like getting dressed or combing my hair. I just slow down and breathe, sit still, and listen. Different breathing techniques give me something to focus on. Sometimes, I "involuntarily" go into a meditative state, say, when I'm waiting in line at a store. Or if I'm stressed, in heavy traffic, and the knucklehead in front of me doesn't take off when the light turns green, I just take a few breaths to calm down and center myself.

On the days I DON'T meditate, I notice I am so much quicker to judge people, drop into negative self-talk, and become impatient. When I do meditate, whether it's for several minutes or even a few seconds, there's a calmness and a confidence boost where I feel at ease in the world. There's the presence of trust. And then something amazing happens, or it doesn't. **Spiritual practice is about creating the space for amazing things to happen.**

> "It is often the space inside the vessel or the doorway which seems of no substance and no value, which, in the end, is the most valuable part of all."
>
> —*Solala Towler*

WHAT KEEPS US FROM MEDITATING?

One thing that frustrates people about meditation is the uninterrupted onslaught of internal dialogue when they sit. That's because **meditation is a window through which to observe the patterns of the things you say to yourself.**

Many of those things are not pretty—sometimes even overwhelming and shame-making. So, you sit for a little bit, and the inner dialogue begins: *Why am I meditating? What is this even about, anyway? I have shit to do. WTF? I suck at meditation—I don't even know how to do it...* And you stop (at least, I did, at first).

In the beginning, even if you practice for two to three minutes, that's good. Eventually, the voices become less aggressive. You can sit longer and longer. The voices become more helpful. You can observe them without attachment, and mysteriously, they shift from scary and negative to positive and sometimes beyond what you could have ever imagined.

In his book *12 Rules for Life,* Canadian clinical psychologist Jordan Peterson shares this gem: "Treat yourself like someone you are responsible for helping," which emphasizes the importance of self-care and self-respect, urging people to care for themselves with the same attention and compassion they would offer to others.

Meditation promotes health, well-being, and peace of mind, and it's at the core of my go-to self-care practices.

PROCRASTINATION IS THE ENEMY OF ACTION

The message is simple: **Don't procrastinate.** We all invent ways to procrastinate taking action toward our goals, dreams, and a life of love. We wait for the "perfect timing" to start a business, get healthier, apologize to a loved one we've hurt, make meditation a practice, finally leave the girlfriend who threw all of our belongings in the front yard and turned on the sprinklers... or publish that book.

Fear is the #1 cause of procrastination. Fear creeps in, taking all kinds of forms—FOMO (fear of missing out), FOPO (fear of other people's opinions), fear of failure, fear of success, and on and on. Well, try out this different take on fear from Stephen Pressfield:

> "Are you paralyzed by fear? That's a good sign. Fear is good. Like self-doubt, fear is an indicator. Fear tells us what we have to do. The more scared we are of a work or calling, the more sure we can be that we HAVE to do it."
>
> —Stephen Pressfield

So, follow your fear faithfully. Wait, what? What I mean by "faith" here is the confidence that you're meant to be exactly where you are in life, moment to moment. It's the faith that you are right where you need to be right now (fear or no fear)—and **faith that your journey so far has sufficiently prepared you for what's next.**

The kind of faith I'm talking about inspires action! With faith, you can accept the personal choices you want to make that will take you where you want to go. You can see your gifts and make them Superpowers. You can tap into those possibilities beyond the current reality to shape your life and make the choices that matter—choices that are meaningful and joyful and good.

My Number One fear over the last five years has been about publishing this book, mainly afraid that it would be misunderstood. Every time that fear comes up as I'm writing, I have to laugh at myself for missing that this is *exactly* the whole point! My message is meant to help you power YOUR passion in pursuit of YOUR potential—with faith and facing the fear.

Thankfully, humor comes to my rescue every time, helping me realize that I am taking meaningful action on what I believe matters. If publishing this book could potentially help millions, AND if it only helps one person, it's worth it. I guess I've already "won" because the one person who is undoubtedly being transformed by this work is, of course, ME. That's the beauty of taking action toward your dreams and goals!

Besides humor, **the best way to overcome your fear is to practice.**

> **My long-time friend, Chris Murphy, is not afraid** to grab the mic at any event. He speaks publicly on a regular basis and plays in a band that does local shows almost every weekend. One time, we were in Atlanta and went to this karaoke place called Metalsome. Murphy hopped on stage first and

sang Billy Idol's "White Wedding" *because* he had never practiced it before! Of course, he nailed it. Another time, we took over a piano bar in Chicago, coercing the piano player to let Murphy play during his break. He had the whole place singing "Bennie and the Jets" at the top of their lungs and was cheered into doing an encore.

I asked Murphy if he ever got nervous going up on stage. He smiled and said, "A little bit. But then, when I get up there, I remember I know eighty-five songs."

This is what you call practice! It takes 80% of the fuel to launch the rocket, but once it gets free of Earth's gravity, it only takes the other 20% to get to the moon. The same is true of practice, whether it's meditation or anything else. Early-stage practice is clunky and funky sometimes. Once you get going, though, it's like riding a bike.

PRACTICE IS ENOUGH WHEN YOU PRACTICE THE RIGHT STUFF

Indeed, practice can become its own reward, a challenging but deeply satisfying activity. Practice is enough because when you continually practice the basics of anything, the result is that **you can make very difficult things look easy.** And more than that, you are often assisted by agencies that seem to come from beyond the ordinary self.

These spontaneous openings or awakenings, whether you call them the Graces of God, the Bhodidarma mind, or the flow of the Great Tao—all of these answer the call for a greater life and confirm our aspirations. **And the feeling of an opening or awakening is priceless.**

In *God and the Evolving Universe: The Next Step in Personal Evolution,* authors James Redfield, Michael Murphy and Sylvia Timbers present a message of hope and a vision for the future. It is no accident, they argue, that the twentieth and early twenty-first centuries have witnessed a revolution in new human capacities. Daily, we hear and read about supernormal athletic feats, clairvoyant perception, lives transformed by meditative practices, and healing through prayer—and we, ourselves, experience these things. The authors contend that thousands of years of human striving have delivered us to this very moment, in which **each act of self-development is creating a new stage in planetary evolution**—and the emergence of a human species possessed of vastly expanded potential.

What's there to fear when the rewards are so great?!

THE PAYOFF: PRINCIPLES OF PRACTICE

We've talked about the practice of freedom and the practice of meditation, and here we are at the practice of choice and action. How are you going to BE in the world using the Action Lens?

Three powerful, patient practices of the principles:

1. ***Call on your inner voice*** to guide you in clarifying your values because your values matter when you are about to make a choice or take an action. Questions you might ask yourself:
    - What is it important to BE right now?
    - How do I choose the language to communicate my message to the world (including body, energy and metaphorical language)?
    - How might I recognize when I am not living in alignment with my highest values?
    - What helps me get back on track?

2. ***Carefully commit to your choice or action***—and mean it. Make sure you nail it spiritually, emotionally, mentally, and in the next steps you take.

3. ***Do what needs to be done*** when it needs to be done, whether you want to or not. Remember, you are only as good as your word—and your word can be hard to hear sometimes. Social pressure and your mind's messaging will have their ups and downs. Make the distinction between inner voice and social hypnosis.

4. ***Choose to act on things you can influence*** in a given situation. There are always factors that are out of your control. When you choose to act on the factors you CAN influence, the number of factors out of your control starts to diminish.

> "Whether you face reality head on and make a life change, or deny your responsibility, you've made a choice. The way I see it, you choose either a life of abundant strength and energy, or you're living in the gap, far beneath the quality of life you could be enjoying."
>
> —*Shawn Phillips*

HERE'S THE (INTER)CONNECTION

When you practice for the sake of the process of practice itself, you find that perfection seems silly to even consider.

How's that again?

Here's what happens: Patient practice generates a natural space for growth and steps around the perfection trap. When you consistently practice doing what you said you were going to do and in the space of growth, fear doesn't feel like part of the equation and eventually drops off.

Self-trust begins to expand and support everything you do. Practicing something new may feel uncomfortable, risky, or uncertain, but you know in that "inner knowing" way that you'll be okay; you have faith that motivates you to take action and focus on the place you're going to be as a result of consistent practice.

Self-trust translates into expanded mutual trust and intimacy in your relationships. You carry your values, integrity, creativity, intellect, and the power of choice into the world. **You represent the honest essence of who you are through how you** *communicate to others, the choices you make, and the actions you take.*

So, what are you waiting for? No time like the present to start practicing—at home with your family, out with your friend, at work with your team, boss, employees, or clients. Time to go out and BE ...!

WRAPPIN' IT UP

> "So, what should we do? Anything, something, as long as we don't just sit there. If we screw up, start over. Try something else. Do anything, even if it's wrong. If it's wrong, fix it. If we wait until we've satisfied all of the uncertainties, it may be too late."
>
> —Lee Iacocca

I worked for Chrysler from 1992 to 1997 as a Certified Gold Sales Associate. The certification process involved computer courses (it was before "online," so I don't remember now what they could have been about!). I wrote down this statement from Iacocca in my Sales Planner Journal during one of the courses, and I still, to this day, come back to read it sometimes to make sure I'm living out his point.

I agree with Lee! Action is where it's at. As we saw in Chapter Three, speaking our world into existence is a powerful thought process nourished by faith, hope, and love. But it doesn't mean much if no action is taken.

It's all in the choice you make, and you own that choice. Now, it's time to find out if money really does grow on trees ...

GOING DEEPER

Breaking Through Procrastination (Using 3x5 Cards)

This practice helps rewire your mindset around procrastination by using affirmations written on 3x5 cards. You will create personalized, empowering statements to shift from delay to action.

Materials Needed:

- A stack of 3x5 index cards
- A pen or markers
- (Optional) Stickers, colors, or symbols for extra motivation

Step 1: Set Your Intention (1 minute)

Take a deep breath and reflect on an area where procrastination holds you back. Ask yourself:

- *What fears or beliefs are keeping me stuck?*
- *How do I want to feel instead?*
- *What action do I want to take today?*

Step 2: Write 5-10 Affirmations (5 minutes)

On each 3x5 card, write one affirmation in the present tense as if it's already true. Use strong, positive language. Here are some examples:

1. *I take action with confidence and ease.*
2. *Every step I take brings me closer to my goal.*
3. *I start now, and momentum carries me forward.*
4. *I am disciplined, focused, and productive.*
5. *I release perfectionism and embrace progress.*
6. *My time is valuable, and I use it wisely.*
7. *I trust myself to complete what I start.*
8. *Taking action feels good, and I welcome it.*
9. *I break tasks into small steps and start with the first one.*
10. *I am unstoppable when I commit to action.*

Step 3: Activate the Affirmations (1 minute)

Hold each card and read it aloud with conviction. Feel the words sink in. Visualize yourself already living this truth. Notice the physical sensations of holding this space.

Step 4: Placement & Daily Practice

- Place your cards where you'll see them often—on your desk, mirror, or even carry one in your pocket.
- Each morning, pick one affirmation to focus on throughout the day.

- Before starting a task, read an affirmation aloud to set the right mindset.

Consistent affirmations will shift your thinking, making action feel natural and an effortless expression of who you are. Ready to take the first step?

NOTES

INNERCHAPTER
FDA APPROVES FIRST MEDITATION PILL (A PARODY)

(Principle of pill as piss poor practice)

Highly confidential and exciting announcement: The meditation pill is *finally* here! No longer will we have to engage in the exploration of profound mystery and uncovering layers of our authentic selves.

Today, the U.S. Food and Drug Administration approved **ZeneXt-C**, an oral solution that contains a purified drug substance derived from the chemicals and hormones known to be associated with the practice of meditation. The FDA has approved this drug for the treatment of patients who don't believe they have time for a five-to-seven-minute daily practice.

ZeneXt-C is a chemical compound that appears in the brains of practitioners who experience the profound beauty and awe of being present in the moment, more commonly known as inner stillness, equanimity, or peace. ZeneXt-C does not cause intoxication. The euphoria is produced through natural brain chemicals and hormonal compounds.

"This approval serves as a reminder that advancing sound development programs that properly evaluate active ingredients contained in marijuana can lead to important medical therapies. The FDA is committed to this kind of careful scientific research and drug development," said FDA Commissioner Mark Gottmeds, M.D.

"Controlled clinical trials, testing the safety and efficacy of the drug, along with careful review through the FDA's drug approval process, are the most appropriate ways to bring meditation-derived treatments to patients. Because of the extensive, well-controlled clinical studies that supported this approval, prescribers can have confidence in the drug's uniform strength."

Innovation drives progress. When it comes to innovation in the development of new drugs and therapeutic biological products, the FDA's Center for Drug Evaluation and Research (CDER) supports the pharmaceutical industry at every step of the process. With its understanding of the science used to create new products, testing and manufacturing procedures, and the diseases and conditions that new products are designed to treat, the FDA provides the scientific and regulatory advice needed to bring new therapies to market.

The company releasing this innovative product cannot be named at this time.

[end transmission]

If you really want the real scoop on meditation, here it is.

There's a lot of talk and research about flow states right now (including from me). Jamie Wheal is an author I heard speak about working on the Flow Genome Project, and **they're looking for the *gene for "flow."***

As much as I respect science, for me, this is completely counterintuitive and defeats the purpose of nothing less than the exploration and profound mystery of uncovering layers of our authentic selves! It's the total Western pathology of creating a "fix" to something for which there's no shortcut, nor should there be. Don't get to the root cause; just paste it over with a pill!

Meditation is part of the beautiful practice of being in flow. The experience itself—setting the intention, practicing, getting better and deeper little by little, being present to the surprises that pop up and to the richness of awareness, as well as the times it doesn't work out (you can't concentrate, you feel stupid doing it, etc.). These are all part of the living, organic package.

Would you want to take a meditation pill? Hey, maybe you would! No judgment.

> *"Best thing to do is nothing."* — Hippocrates

CHAPTER FIVE

ECONOMIC LENS— PROFESSION

Put the ECO back in Economics

hilosophy is nice, but you gotta eat.

In Part One, we developed a skill to see things differently through the Spiritual, Emotional, Mental, and Action Lenses. From this foundation of self-exploration and discovery, we now dive into the ways in which we interact with the external world.

What better place to start than work and money??

Putting the ECO back in economics calls us to harmonize our work with scientific, natural, and spiritual principles. Our six extraordinary human gifts will illuminate the path toward a livelihood that nourishes our souls—one of material sustenance, mental clarity, emotional well-being, and spiritual fulfillment.

Imagine your work as a fresh tapestry, which you weave with every choice you make to build and align your occupation with your values and aspirations.

> Jane was an attorney in a high-paying job she thought she loved, but she discovered it was draining her emotionally and spiritually. Her six senses gave her the signals—she often felt fatigued and had consistent aches and pains that couldn't be diagnosed. Her inner voice gently whispered, *Why don't you reconsider your career path*? With imagination and a little humor (to tamp down her fears and doubts), she began to open her mind to another way of using her talents, and identified what things and experiences she felt most passionate about.
>
> Jane ultimately made the courageous choice to leave her job and transition into a field focused on environmental conservation. Her new position blended all of her talents and six human gifts, brought her profound fulfillment and purpose, a healthier lifestyle—and adequately served her financial needs.

Choice empowers you to craft a career that resonates with your innermost desires. It's the compass that guides you toward professions that nurture your spirit and the world around you.

It's what moves you forward toward the decisions and actions that keep you on the path.

Imagination fuels your ability to envision an ideal livelihood that sustains you financially and enriches your soul. It calls you to dream beyond conventional career boundaries and discover innovative ways to contribute to society while finding personal satisfaction.

Inner voice serves as a wise companion, guiding you through this imaginative landscape. You develop the patterns of thought that will take you forward, not hold you back, or maintain a status quo that doesn't serve you.

Self-awareness wakes you up to recognize when your current livelihood strays from your authentic path and to make course corrections when needed.

Sensation of the six senses alerts you to the physical sensations that arise when your livelihood is in harmony or dissonance with your values. As you navigate the complexities of work, these sensations serve as valuable cues, guiding you toward choices that honor your well-being and spiritual growth.

Humor (maybe the most underestimated gift of all when it comes to the world of work!) infuses joy into your pursuit of career and financial goals. It allows you to laugh at your missteps, find levity in the face of challenges, and maintain resilience on this profound journey.

WE ARE PLANTS AND PLANETS

For most of us, our everyday lives revolve around work and money—paying the bills, getting the promotion, making the sale, and feathering the nest egg for the future. This pursuit can be pretty time-consuming and nerve-wracking, leaving little room for much else and, ultimately, becoming so consuming that it saps our energy and our joy.

> "No one on his deathbed ever said, 'I wish I had spent more time on my business.'"
>
> —Arnold Zack, sent in a 1983 letter to his friend, Sen. Paul Tsongas

Just beyond a bustling city, where the pace of life seemed to mimic the relentless grind of machines, I was studying for a graduate degree at JFK University in Orinda, CA, a short tunnel ride to the cities of Oakland and San Francisco. A philosophy about the human condition and economics began to develop for me, as I had recently learned a curious perspective on life: that humans are more akin to plants and planets than to cold, mechanical contraptions like machines.

One day, as I strolled through the lush botanical gardens at Golden Gate Park, the concept began to unfold for me. I marveled at the similarities between humans and plants. Just like plants seeking sunlight, humans yearn for warmth and connection. They root themselves in communities and flourish when nurtured by love and kindness.

On another night, I gazed up at the night sky from the deck of a houseboat on Lake Shasta. Much like celestial bodies, I thought about how humans are interconnected in a vast cosmic dance. Our actions ripple through the fabric of society, impacting the lives of others in ways we can't always fathom.

In the years that followed, my musings began to extend to the world of business. A company is not a cold, mechanical entity driven solely by profit; it's a living ecosystem teeming with diverse talents, ideas, and ambitions. Employees are like the leaves of a tree, absorbing knowledge and energy from the environment. Leaders act as caretakers, ensuring the well-being of the ecosystem.

Now, my operational model is this: **A business is more than the sum of its parts, just as a forest is more than a collection of trees. It thrives when each component is nurtured, just as humans flourish when connected to serving the greater world.**

In the grand tapestry of life, we are not cogs in a machine but *vibrant participants in a complex living system.* Just as plants seek light and planets orbit stars, humans are unique creatures that seek purpose and connection. And in the bustling ecosystem of business, success is not measured by profit alone but by the flourishing of its people and the positive impact it creates in the world.

ECOSYSTEM VALUES FOR SUSTAINABLE SYSTEMS-BASED SOLUTIONS

If you try to explain what a bird is by naming its characteristics, you come up with a list: beak, feathers, wings, flies through the air. You could say, "Okay, that's a bird." But then someone shows up with a pile of feathers, a beak, and wings and tosses it all up in the air and says, "It's a bird!" *And it's not a bird at all!*

Moral: *If you don't understand and incorporate the laws of nature in your design, all you have is a pile of feathers.*

If a business is a living system, the same principles apply to its systems, processes and culture. **Design all of your systems with the Laws of Nature at the forefront.**

If you already visualize business as a living system, welcome to the fold! If you're wondering how to live it every day, it's all about walky-walky...

Here are my Top Ten recommendations for actions that will nurture your business system, support your people, build your relationships, help the work, and make you money!

1. **Define your values and mission.** Establish clear values and a mission statement that reflect your organization's purpose and principles as a foundation for decision-making and alignment within the ecosystem. Uphold ethical standards in all your operations, which include fair treatment of employees, honest marketing, and responsible financial practices. You'll see my

company's *"Ecology of Values"* in the Innerchapter that follows this one.

2. **Prioritize employee well-being.** Offer a supportive workplace *culture* that values work-life balance, mental health, and personal growth. Engaged and satisfied employees contribute positively to the ecosystem.

3. **Use a customer-centric approach.** Focus on understanding and meeting the needs of your customers. Build relationships, gather *feedback,* and continually improve your products/services to create loyal customers who contribute to the ecosystem.

4. **Invest in learning and development** to expand your employees' ongoing knowledge and skills. This benefits your organization and *enriches* the talent pool within the ecosystem.

5. **Model and encourage transparent and open communication.** Share information about company goals, strategies, and challenges. Encourage feedback and *dialogue* at all levels.

6. **Implement sustainable practices** that reduce environmental impact, such as *energy* efficiency, waste reduction, and responsible sourcing. Sustainability efforts will improve the planet and also *resonate* positively with customers and partners—and maybe save you money in the long run!

7. **Measure and evaluate impact.** Regularly assess the impact of your business on your customer-supplier-strategic partner *ecosystem*. Use key performance indicators (KPIs) to gauge progress and make data-driven decisions.

8. **Adopt a long-term perspective** in your decision-making. Consider the sustainability and *resilience* of your business and its impact on the entire ecosystem.

9. **Seed and support startups and small businesses.** Nurture the *growth* of startups and small businesses within your ecosystem. They often bring fresh ideas and can contribute to economic vitality.

10. **Engage in your community** by considering how your business can positively impact it. Support local causes, collaborate with nearby businesses, and contribute to community development. Generously serve a community with your *time, talent, and treasure*.

P.S. These Top Ten put into play all my unique human gifts, sometimes challenging my beliefs and bringing my life fulfillment every single day. Work and play, business and pleasure, and work-life balance—all of these concepts that used to keep my life and work separate have become boundless.

It's awesome!

WHAT ECONOMICS LOOKS LIKE: "WASTE EQUALS FOOD" APPROACH

The cradle-to-grave or "waste equals food" approach to business represents a paradigm shift in companies' operations. It emphasizes sustainability, circularity, and responsible resource management. In this approach, companies aim to minimize waste and environmental impact while maximizing the efficiency of resources throughout their entire lifecycle.

> **One of my largest clients is a forward-thinking grocery chain** that strategically purchases large wholesale goods, including fresh produce, at discounted rates. Rather than discarding items nearing their expiration date, they redistribute them to local charities and food banks, ensuring that surplus food doesn't go to waste.
>
> They prioritize sourcing products from environmentally conscious suppliers with sustainable farming and packaging practices. The savings from these efficiencies are passed on to customers through competitive pricing.

This example demonstrates how businesses can adopt a cradle-to-grave mindset, where every resource is thoughtfully managed from its creation to its eventual reuse or recycling. And another precious benefit: Employees love that their work has meaning beyond the paycheck—they're contributing to something bigger than themselves that's healthy for the planet and for their children and children's children!

Try ECOnomical win-win-win strategies in your business to embrace the principles of sustainability, efficiency, and social responsibility.

IT'S "FREEDOM WITH THE FLOW" THAT COUNTS

When I was nineteen, my "lens" was money. Sure, I had dreams of being a pro baseball player and a medical doctor, but my focus was on whatever would make money. I worked full-time for a residential construction company while majoring in Business at Sacramento State.

One day, Bart, one of our subcontractors, asked me on his way out the door, "Hey, do you ever listen to business tapes?" I answered, *"Hell yeah!"* while, at the same time, thinking, *"WTF is a business tape?"* My driven personality had me at "business."

He tossed the tape to me, and I listened to the whole thing on my way home in the cassette player of my S-10 Blazer (if you need to know what a cassette player is, Google it—they were awesome).

The tape's title was *The Law of Time and Money*, and it explained how good business models don't depend on trading time for money. It also gave a general outline and description of a specific business opportunity that was currently available and recommended that I contact the person who gave me the tape if I wanted to learn more.

I had miraculously found the fast track to the promised land of vast and immediate financial success!

The business op turned out to be Amway Products. Once they dispelled the myth that Amway was a scam and described a "bulletproof" method based on duplication similar to how Ray Kroc sold hamburgers, I was interested. By the time it came down to signing up and paying $100 for a start-up kit ($97 if it were marketed today online), I was IN 110%.

Here I was, part of a billion-dollar global company with 300 manufacturers, 15,000 products, and a proven training system. How rad is that for a nineteen-year-old? I immediately sponsored a few people and thought, *"This is so cool. I'll be an Amway Diamond in three years, living financially free on the beaches of the world!"*

Well, I didn't end up making millions from this business because I wasn't emotionally mature enough to understand what the true success of Amway was based on. It was less about selling, selling, selling and more about *helping others achieve their dreams*. I didn't take advantage of the resources (like my sponsor Bart's help) that were committed to my success because I was focused on my own success—another "inside-out" aha. ***I had to build my relationship with myself before I could build relationships with others to build a business.***

I did take away Amway's blueprint for NOT trading time for money, which I've modified over the years to grow my businesses and help others start and grow theirs. Here's the quick Hiddle-Haddle version of their eight-step keys to the kingdom of business-building success:

1. **Hand out business tapes**, which means prospecting—put yourself out there and make those calls because you have a purpose and passion for what you're doing. Build meaningful contacts and relationships, giving people something so they want to learn more.
2. **Show the plan**, outline your goals, value proposition, growth plan, etc., for yourself and with your people.
3. **Use the product**, which is about integrity and belief in the value of what you offer. Using the product is a metaphor for how you walk your talk in every area of your life, from the foods you eat, to what you use to bathe, to how you get to and from work.
4. **Work with your sponsor (Bart!)**, mentor, and anyone who can help you move forward. Learn from the successes and failures of others.
5. **Sell some product**, work your funnel unapologetically, price well, deliver well, and reap the rewards!
6. **Read self-help books and listen to tapes** because personal growth is essential to your ECOnomics and happiness.

7. **Attend conferences and seminars** that will offer you more growth and exposure to other successful people and knowledge.
8. **Associate with like-minded people**; get out and network actively to build connections, relationships, and resources. You never know what sales opportunities are out there if you don't look. (More on relationships and alliances in *Chapter Nine*.)

My best friend, Dan, specializes in General Liability Workers' Compensation insurance for contractors. He's one of the most brilliant people in the world and a natural sales guy. *He does five times the volume of anyone else in his office, working the least amount of hours!* He takes the most time off and is rated near the top nationally on client retention—his policy renewal rates are over 90%, which is unheard of in the industry.

How does he do it? He LIVES the eight steps to success. He knows his stuff and is passionate about the service he's offering his clients and their workers. He is not selling insurance; he's building relationships. He's an ally, coach and partner with his clients to understand the information, find the best coverage, and get the paperwork done. He is continually adapting and innovating to get ahead.

Dan sees the interrelationships of his business within the grand tapestry of life; his clients aren't cogs in a machine but participants in a living system. He gets a lot of referrals, and when clients do go elsewhere, they often return because of the extraordinary value he adds to their business.

MONEY: WHEN IS IT "ENOUGH"?

Thankfully, I grew out of that nineteen-year-old all-about-money mindset. Money's still important; it's just not that important in the grand ecosystem scale of things. I've learned that meaningful relationships, enjoying quality time, and becoming a better businessperson and a better dad, husband and friend are the most important things. And, lo and behold, I'm making more money today, making more impact, and having much more fun than ever before!

Falling in love with money is like falling in love with an inch— it's just a conceptual measure of something abstract.

Moral: Set a limit, or enough is NEVER enough.

It's easy to get addicted to money. I know. I was there. Setting a limit on financial goals is essential because pursuing endless wealth can lead to a never-ending cycle of unfulfilled desire and lifelong discontent.

Here's an idea: *Identify and strive for a high financial target, then commit to giving away the surplus!* You begin to shift your focus from mindless accumulation to purposeful living.

The benefits abound! You feel the immense power of sharing abundance; it brings you a sense of fulfillment, gratitude, and the knowledge that you have done something generous to help others. It's not like you are selling yourself short or committing to "lose." You are adopting a mindset that stimulates a more balanced and compassionate relationship with wealth, benefiting both you and society as a whole.

It's less about the specific limit we set and more about recognizing that "enough" exists.

PAYOFF: NEXT-LEVEL TIPS FOR YOUR OPERATIONAL ECOSYSTEM

1. Innovate continuously to serve selflessly. Innovation in business doesn't just mean what you do to introduce new goods and services. A leader must explore personal innovation to stay relevant in a dynamic business environment and interconnected world.

Optimize your potential to solve important problems with replicable, regenerative solutions. Shoot higher so you can contribute to projects you feel make a difference.

How do you do it? Start by asking yourself: *What positive innovation did I make this year that has made a difference in service? What might I see or do that's even better?*

> **Ray Kroc was a milkshake mixer traveling salesman** who opened his eyes to opportunity. He could have seen the success of the McDonald brothers as a way to sell more milkshake machines, but he

chose to look at the whole pattern of their business model. He convinced the McDonald brothers to expand their business and, in the process, he created a completely new way of doing business. Ray Kroc didn't invent the hamburger, but he understood how the duplication process could sell a shitload of them.

Be open to change and continually seek ways to evolve. Begin by looking at your go-to paradigms. If you're living in the current social and economic structure (which we are), you likely identify with "strategic command and control" leadership.

News flash: We are all consciously co-evolving away from command-and-control toward more mindful and people-centered paradigms. The rigid, top-down approach, where leaders dictate with little input, is not cutting it anymore. The more innovative leader values collaboration, empowerment, and empathy, with the intention to promote a workplace where people feel motivated to contribute creatively and authentically. Among the paradigm concepts floating around in recent days are "servant leadership," "transformational leadership," "adaptive leadership," and "conscious leadership."

This framework represents a transformational shift that attempts to see reality as an evolving pattern, not a fixed set of strictly material realities. Its purpose is to go beyond today's individual strategies through accelerated cross-pollination of significant leadership values.

Evolve your tools as your systems evolve (and vice versa). Innovations in renewable energy, sustainable materials, and smart manufacturing help companies align profit with environmental goals and regulatory standards (and often, reduce costs). Automation and data analytics can streamline operations, reduce waste, and optimize resource use. At this point in history, the power of tools like AI—like it or not—are transforming the way businesses get things done, and the way our world works.

In the last few years, I've been rethinking how I can build relationships that will best serve my clients and make our business more profitable. The innovative tool that changed things for me was the podcast—first listening to people I learned from and/or wanted to connect with, and then hosting one myself.

> **For a long time, I believed podcasts were** just a time-suck, but I soon found that listening to podcasts was a great way to learn fast and connect to others who share your passions. I've been learning from some of the best thought leaders and innovators, which is how I met John Corcoran (former White House Writer in Presidential Letters and Messages for President Bill Clinton) and then Dr. Jeremy Weisz, co-founders of Rise 25. Their company helps B2B businesses get more clients, referral partners, and strategic partners through their podcast service.
>
> These guys brilliantly shared with me all the benefits of podcasting, including how I could leverage my time and use podcasting as a tool that could

radically multiply my personal reach, optimizing my potential to build a business.

Now I host my own podcast, called the *Tao of Pizza,* of course! It's been a great way to show up in the ecosystem and expand my network in a manner that only podcasts can do. I can also recycle podcast content into other tools that offer value and make connections, such as courses, talks, eBooks, and books.

And it's working fantastic for me. Recently, I was referred to a potential client whose COO, Martin, agreed to meet with me. I walked into the office a little nervous because the stakes were so high. I was introduced to Martin, and the first thing he said was, "Hey, I checked out your podcast. It's pretty cool." I felt like he was selling to *me*, not the other way around! The podcast is a way for people to get to know me, like a business card on steroids. Bonus: If they don't like what they hear in the podcast, then we both avoid the time and hassle of figuring out we're not a fit.

2. Build a network of trust-based alliances. The more we nurture business relationships, the more successful the entire business ecosystem will become—not to mention your company's bottom line and your personal well-being! Collaborations can lead to innovation, expanded networks, and mutually beneficial opportunities. Seek collaborative and strategic partnerships with other businesses and organizations.

When people ask me how I started and built my company, my recurring thought is, *it wasn't me*. As my career unfolded and I focused on building a trust-based relationship ecosystem, starting a business evolved naturally from a lifelong dream to a no-brainer step into a new role in business as an owner/entrepreneur, and from there, growing a successful business that supports my family, allows me to enjoy life and gives me the chance to make a difference in the world.

I sure didn't do it alone, and there's just no way I could have planned or created where I am today. Relationships start with planting a seed to connect, without expectations or judgments. It's not a zero-sum game where you make forty contacts a day for forty days and then tick off the returns on each one. **Building a network of trust-based alliances is a nonlinear, dynamic, and fluid process (sounds very Tao, doesn't it?).** And it works.

Many of the experts I've referred to and quoted in this book are from those trusted alliances—and close friendships—that have helped me along the way.

While I was working as a territory manager for a material handling company, Gilbert was a competitor-supplier whom I got to know very well over eight years. He got in the habit of calling me every Tuesday at 4:30 because he knew I was on my way home, worn out after sitting all day in our weekly corporate meetings. He'd say to me, "Write me a check for $800 because that's how much you're losing by not owning your own company. It's ridiculous for you to do this when you could work for yourself!"

Another supplier, my good friend Ron, told me, "C'mon, grow a pair of balls. Take a second on your house and start your own company! We will supply you with the inventory because you don't need anything to sell at first. We will help you build a good company. You're ready!"

I knew all of this was true, but they were the ones who helped me believe I could do it and trusted me enough to help me through it. We collaborated on projects in those early years of my new business, and I wouldn't have been able to do it on my own.

And then there's my friend, Chris Murphy...

> **Call it fate: I quit my job** on the fifteenth (payday seemed a logical choice), wrote a class-act letter to my boss with gratitude for everything I had learned from him (which was a fair amount), and walked away with a huge commission check to start my own company. I knew I had to have an attorney to do the corporate stuff, but I didn't know much else.
>
> Remember my friend, the musician, who taught me how to overcome fear by practicing? Chris Murphy had been encouraging me for a long time to start my own business. He didn't know I had made this decision, yet he happened to show up at my doorstep on that very day—the universe was conspiring for my success! As soon as I opened the door, I blurted out, "Hey, dude, I started a company!"

He replied, "Wow, do you have a website?" I responded (probably with the look of a deer in the headlights), "No, I have no idea how to do that." Murphy brushed past me into the house, set up his computer on the dining-room table, and within minutes, bought me three domain names (all of which I use to this day). I had no idea what a domain name was, but I knew it was a great move, not to mention the fact that it made this new adventure *very* real.

Murphy is mentioned several times in this book because our relationship has evolved from business to serving on the Warehousing Education and Research Council together for a decade. As president of Sierra Pacific Warehouse Group, he's a top customer. He's also a close friend, fellow volunteer, Magic Man, and part of my chosen family.

I feel grateful to know that I've also been a good influence on other people, helping them accomplish things they might not have been able to do alone. Micah was a young forklift sales associate I took under my wing for a few years; he went off on his own and recently sold his company for close to eight figures.

Sebastian is a friend I met through his father, and at the time, he was making extra money trimming weed in his garage because he wanted to be a stay-at-home dad. When I discovered his business background (not trimming weed, but five years of doing CAD drawings for a large company in our industry), I suggested we meet to discuss potential business opportunities.

Within weeks, he started doing projects for us as a consultant. Then, I began introducing him to some of my clients who could also benefit from his services. Sebastian went from a good side hustle to owning a six-figure company, where he does engineering, consulting, and permit processing while developing a business model that still allowed him to spend valuable time raising his children. I love this guy—a family man who's a wild card, funny, and has become an important strategic partner to my business.

The beauty of these stories is that these relationships emerged out of caring and sharing, not for the goal of making money, although they did turn out to be profitable for everybody. It's the balance of peace and profit!

3. Share success. Celebrate achievements and share success stories, both internally and externally. One of the best supports an employee or team can receive is celebrating a job well done. Everybody's lifted up with shared success. Positive narratives can inspire others and strengthen the ecosystem's reputation.

HERE'S THE (INTER)CONNECTION

True success in work and business isn't just about profit margins and bottom lines—it's about aligning our careers with our values, nurturing our personal, professional, and community ecosystems, and creating a life in which our work nourishes our financial bottom line AND our soul.

I mentioned earlier my volunteer time with the Warehousing Education and Research Council (WERC), a division of the Material Handling Industry (MHI). Michael Mikitka is WERC's executive vice president, and WERC is a founding member and industry partner of the American Logistics Aid Network (ALAN). I had the pleasure of hosting him on my podcast, where he shared how collaboration among individuals, businesses and government can save lives.

> **In the bustling world of warehousing and logistics**, where time is of the essence and precision is paramount, ALAN is an association of industries that come together to spring into action when disaster strikes. Its origin comes from Hurricane Katrina in 2005, a challenge unlike anything most disaster relief professionals had ever faced—a logistics nightmare. Afterward, people got together to work on how they could do better the next time a disaster like this hit in terms of coordinating the logistics and services needed to bring relief and accelerate recovery.
>
> One fateful day, a massive storm ravaged a major logistics hub, threatening to disrupt supply chains and leave countless businesses in turmoil. ALAN swiftly activated its network of volunteers,

coordinating efforts to deliver essential supplies, restore power, and provide much-needed support.

Dedicated warehouse managers, truck drivers, and logistics experts from across the nation rallied to the cause, working tirelessly to rebuild what the tempest had torn asunder. They loaded trucks with critical goods, navigated treacherous terrain, and offered a lifeline to those in need.

Through their relentless dedication and collaboration, ALAN and its army of industry heroes demonstrated that the logistics world could unite, even in the face of adversity, to provide swift and effective assistance.

Stories like these illuminate how our six extraordinary human gifts can guide us toward a fulfilling livelihood. These gifts empower us to craft careers that financially sustain us *and* enrich our lives profoundly.

By viewing businesses as living ecosystems rather than cold, mechanical entities, we've highlighted the importance of designing systems and cultures that respect and incorporate the laws of nature. Success, in this context, is measured not by profit alone but by relationships flourishing, the health of our communities, and the positive impact we make on the world.

We've also reflected on the journey from a money-centric mindset to one that recognizes the true wealth found in relationships, purpose, and contribution. As we innovate, build trust-based alliances, and share our successes, we create a ripple effect that enhances the entire ecosystem.

The new ECOnomics is a sustainable, compassionate, and fulfilling way of living and working in an interconnected world.

WRAPPIN' IT UP

I invite you to rethink your approach to economics and work, and consider pursuing a path that fuels personal growth, environmental stewardship, and social responsibility. By nurturing a business ecosystem that values people, planet, and professional development, you contribute to a holistic and sustainable world that benefits everyone and leaves a positive legacy.

'Nuff said!

GOING DEEPER

"What would I do if I had a million dollars?" Great question to ask yourself, but if you're like me and answered, "Put it in my 401K," you might want to give it some more thought. Let's make it more interesting: *What would I do if money* weren't *an issue?*

Write down the different ways you would spend the money—consider these prompts (and use your gift of imagination to create your own!). You can choose to set your own dollar figure, like ten million:

- Travel and exploration
- Giving back

- Passion and creativity
- Career and purpose
- Relationships and experiences
- Personal growth and well-being

STEPPING INTO ABUNDANCE

As you reflect on your aspirations, notice the deeper desires behind each choice. Your financial prosperity transcends money and includes freedom, purpose, and fulfillment. Imagining a life where money isn't a barrier taps into what truly matters to you.

Take a moment to bridge the gap between vision and reality. *What small steps can I take today to align with this abundant mindset?* Maybe it's setting aside time for a passion project, investing in personal growth, or giving generously in ways that don't require millions.

Financial success isn't just about numbers—it's about living with intention, confidence, and a belief in your ability to create the life you desire. Use this list as a guide, and remind yourself: abundance begins with the ecosystem of relationships, resources, and professional development you cultivate today.

NOTES

INNERCHAPTER
AN ECOLOGY OF VALUES

(Sow the seeds of peace and prosperity)

The Ecology of Values list provides a context for my closest relationships, and I hold myself accountable to living them. It also represents the core values that my company created. I've asked those closest to me to keep me accountable for living these values to create a world with more peace and prosperity for everyone.

THE OPPORTUNITIES WE FACE ARE BIG, SO WE DREAM BIG.
We will never insult the human capacity with small thinking and playing it safe with our gifts. *#VISION*

THE LOCAL COMMUNITY IS A BIG DEAL TO US.
We will invest our lives to build the local community. *#LOCALCOMMUNITY*

WE WILL BE A PLACE FOR PEOPLE TO CONNECT AND EXPERIENCE GREATNESS.
Lives flourish when inspired by something greater than self. *#PRESENCE*

WE WILL FIND OUR SIGNIFICANCE THROUGH RELATIONSHIPS.
We serve our communities well through meaningful connections. *#BELONG*

WE WILL LEAD THE WAY WITH IRRATIONAL GENEROSITY.
We truly practice the principle, "It is better to give than receive." *#GENEROSITY*

WE LOVE OUR PLANET AND WILL TAKE RESPONSIBILITY FOR IT.
Actions speak louder than words. Driving a Prius doesn't count. *#OURPLANET*

OUR #1 RULE IS "ENJOY THE JOURNEY."
We laugh hard, we laugh loud, and we laugh often. *#FUN*

WE ALWAYS BRING OUR BEST.
"We are what we repeatedly do. Excellence, then, is not an act, but a habit." —Aristotle *#EXCELLENCE*

WE ARE LIFELONG LEARNERS.
Always reading, seeking, and pursuing our full potential. *#GROW*

WE CHOOSE TO LOOK FOR THE BIGGER PICTURE.
Taking action locally and globally. *#GO*

"Sow a thought and you reap an action; sow an act and you reap a habit; sow a habit and you reap a character; sow a character and you reap a destiny." —Ralph Waldo Emerson

CHAPTER SIX

EFFORT LENS—PATIENCE
Make it part of your DNA

Making patience part of your DNA is a natural result of embracing and cultivating a Whole Person Paradigm.

We uncover the profound alchemy of **effort—the key to nurturing our mental, action, emotional, and spiritual intelligence** to craft a life of peace, purpose and prosperity. How are we going to use our six extraordinary gifts to serve?

Imagine life as an intricate tapestry woven from the threads of our unique gifts that will create our destiny and life legacy. Consider an example—the decision to maintain a healthier lifestyle.

Jamie experienced a health scare that woke him up to the preciousness of life and health.

He began listening to his inner voice to guide him toward changes he might consider making. Self-awareness and sensation of the six senses taught him to listen to his body, which revealed that bad habits were harming his health. Jamie began to make healthier choices in his diet and monitored his portions. His imagination kicked in as he realized he really liked to cook and create healthy recipes that his family and friends would enjoy. As Jamie realized the beauty and value of a healthier life, his moods lightened, and he began to have more fun in everyday activities and in his relationships.

Choice is the loom upon which we weave the fabric of our existence. As we know, every thought, intention and action constitutes a choice. We are empowered to decide where to direct our efforts, shaping our destiny in the process.

Inner voice whispers guidance, urging us to make choices that align with our well-being, passions, and goals—in the near term and over time as we weave through our journey of life.

Imagination kindles the flame of aspiration. It allows us to envision the best version of ourselves and the path we must tread. Through creativity and vision, we set goals and visualize our journey so that we can manifest our desired future.

Self-awareness provides our compass. It illuminates the terrain of our emotions and thoughts, guiding us toward choices that nurture inner growth. Through self-awareness, we recognize self-defeating patterns and choose to transform them.

Sensation of the six senses grounds us in the wisdom of our bodies. It offers feedback about our physical and emotional state, helping us calibrate our efforts. We listen to our bodies, honoring the need for rest, balance, and rejuvenation.

Humor reminds us not to take life's challenges too seriously, infusing our efforts with joy and resilience. This part of the journey is where the rubber meets the road, and we may face speed bumps and roadblocks along the way. For Jamie, embracing humor looked like this:

> **To adopt a healthier lifestyle, including regular exercise**, Jamie started going to World Class Fitness Gym. He quickly realized it was more challenging than expected. The first few workouts left him sore, exhausted, and feeling self-conscious, like everyone else was judging him. The prospect of returning to the gym became increasingly daunting, and he began to lose resolve.
>
> Then, Jamie got an inspired idea—why succumb to his inner doubts and fears? If you can't beat'em, join'em! He decided to create a "Gym Fails" journal. Instead of dwelling on the struggles and clumsy moments at the gym, Jamie documented these experiences with humor, like when he mistakenly tried to use the rowing machine backward,

or his comically awkward attempts at mastering yoga poses in class.

Recording these mishaps with a humorous twist helped him feel better, and he was reminded that everyone starts somewhere. Jamie realized that even seasoned "gym rats" had their share of awkward moments when they first began (and, he began to notice, still did sometimes).

By injecting humor into the journey of self-improvement through his journal, **Jamie shifted the focus from perfection to progress.** Each gym visit became an opportunity for a new story, making the process less intimidating. Over time, Jamie's efforts at the gym became less about striving for an ideal and more about embracing the imperfect, humorous, and human side of the journey toward a healthier lifestyle.

ACCEPTANCE AND SURRENDER

> "The ability to dominate nature is what many believe to be the secret of security...Now, there's one other great choice, and that is to trust nature and move with it, rather than against it, and to find in that harmony the secret of true civilization."
>
> —Theodore Roszak

Speaking of the gym, you might have heard the axiom "no pain, no gain," and also know that any good fitness trainer today is going to share the shadow side of that concept. Exertion, yes! Pushing outside your comfort zone, yes! Getting to the gym even if you'd rather be lounging on the couch, yes! Even though gain comes with some amount of pain, pain is also a message from your body that something's out of whack. You want to listen to that message and NOT push through the pain. True and lasting results come from sustainable, incremental effort over time.

The same holds true for the Effort Lens. "Effort" is defined in most dictionaries as a vigorous or determined attempt; conscious exertion of power; mental or physical activity needed to achieve something. **Effort is not supposed to require pain or suffering.** However, that's often how people view effort and, for that matter, personal or spiritual growth in general.

So, acceptance, surrender, flow. Does this sound like BS? Well, let's look at it. There's struggle in life. There's suffering. Where's the flow in that? We suffer from all types of things: *Is this deal going to go through? Is she going to stay with me? Will I ever be good enough?*

The key is that some people are suffering and they don't let go. Maybe it's a lost relationship, or they got burned for a lot of money by their partner or accountant. Unhappy things happen, and everyone is entitled to their fair share of suffering over it. At the same time, it can make us feel stuck.

If you hold onto that suffering, there is no energy or focus to move forward. **How much of life might you be missing because you're stuck in suffering?** How much more of life could you experience and enjoy if you chose to accept what is and enter the flow?

Another stuck point is to hold onto your ego, which is "protecting" you by saying you already have everything figured out, and what else could possibly be added to the puzzle (or the pizza)? Have you ever had an experience where you had the chance to try something new, and your ego was yelling loud and clear in your head: *No, that's not safe! You've never tried that before. DON'T DO IT! DON'T GO THERE!*

Say there's an exotic dish on the menu in a restaurant that you *know* you will hate without ever having tasted it before. Your friends finally shame you into trying it. You get pissed off, you dramatically hold your nose, take a bite ... and you say, "Hey... this is delicious!" Multiply that experience to the nth degree, and you'll see how many times your ego has tried to block your efforts, no matter how beneficial they may be to your growth and happiness.

Living through the Effort Lens asks you the question: *What if I stopped struggling against nature?* as Theodore Roszak suggests. *What if I accepted nature and decided to trust it and flow with it?*

Now you're talkin'! **You are surrendering to the truth of Life, which doesn't make you weak; it makes you strong.** You see Life as it is and work with it through all your Lenses and gifts.

> **When it comes to surrender and the ego,** I know whereof I speak. I spent a lot of years thinking I was smart enough to figure everything out on my own. In fact, I was deeply invested in being that way, subconsciously, because I believed I had

something to prove to my dad. The REAL liberation came when I figured out that I needed to surrender. There were some things in my life that had dragged me down—mistakes I'd made, people I'd hurt, destructive things I was holding onto. I was twenty-something and just thought, *Well, that's who I AM. I'm just that kind of person. End of story.*

When I had my first "religious experience," it was an enormous reckoning in which I realized, *Wait a minute. That's NOT who I am.* In most cases, my ego was in charge instead of me, and he was lying to me! Each time I awakened to something new and better, I started to joke with myself: *Damn, I KNEW this! Why didn't I see it before? My ego's keeping it from me!*

I'm almost embarrassed to say that I've been fortunate enough to have four... oops, now five, reckoning experiences (so far), and with each awakening, I surrender a little more to **the reality that I know so much AND I don't know anything at all.** I'm still practicing, learning, and making it look easy :-).

TAKE IT EASY... BUT TAKE IT

Richard Strozzi-Heckler is an amazing person I've been following for years. He is an executive coach, consultant, expert in Somatics, founder of Strozzi Institute, and author of *In Search of the Warrior Spirit: Teaching Awareness Disciplines to the Green Berets.* And this is just the tip of the iceberg of his expertise!

I'm on his email list, and he always closes his newsletters with ***"Take it easy… but take it."*** I love this! It involves all the human gifts and living in the world through all the Lenses we've been talking about. The idea is to accept and make a stand for the things that are important to you. This is not permission to become a couch potato or be wishy-washy about life—quite the opposite!

When we do have pain, struggle, and suffering in our lives, part of acceptance is **not to block or bury these experiences but to embrace healing.**

"Taking it easy, but taking it" is a subtle yet profound shift in perspective that encapsulates the essence of acceptance. Taking it easy is not about avoidance or burying the painful memories. It is about acknowledging them without allowing them to consume your being. This balance becomes a poignant lesson, particularly for anyone facing adversity.

> **One of my best friends is a veteran** on a healing journey with post-traumatic stress disorder (PTSD). We have shared a profound exploration of the themes of acceptance and surrender. His compelling story resembles the struggles many veterans face. I hold deep gratitude for veterans and acknowledge the distinct path my life could have taken, echoing a sentiment shared by those of my generation who did not face mandatory military service or make the choice to serve. Tony's and my bond of trust and acknowledgment sets the stage for this testament to the transformative power of acceptance.

Tony began to open up about his combat experiences, of witnessing the full trauma of war and feeling the guilt of it all. I couldn't imagine what that was like.

Through our discussions, we started to witness the emergence of the theme of acceptance. I supported Tony's courage on the journey toward acknowledging and facing the emotional toll of war. Tony shared how he used to block out the harrowing memories, which is a common strategy to adopt when faced with overwhelming trauma. A kind of, *Yeah, all this crap happened to me, but I'm good. I'll just block it out and take it easy.*

He decided to get coaching at the VA with a methodology that helps clients move from passive acceptance of "I'm okay, you're okay" toward a more proactive approach. Tony learned some new skills around acceptance and surrender through sharing stories, role-playing, and practicing non-judgment. In the process, he found a supportive spiritual community.

Genuine conversations forged a deep connection between Tony and me, providing a healing platform for both of us. We discussed the importance of practicing these newfound skills in the game of life. Tony's journey reflects the broader human experience, where facing challenges head-on with acceptance and surrender becomes the key to personal growth and freedom from suffering.

The nuanced exploration of "taking it easy but taking it" resonates as a **universal lesson in facing adversity with grace, acknowledging pain without succumbing to it, and actively choosing to participate in your life's journey.**

GO WITH THE FLOW STATE

Entering flow states to experience abundance in your life involves cultivating a combination of psychological, emotional, and practical factors. These are internal as well as external practices. By the way, a sense of abundance is not just about external success but also about finding contentment and fulfillment in your pursuits.

Create the container for—and expect—abundance. When you choose to expect abundance based on the conviction that opportunities and possibilities (frequently presented as challenges) are a natural part of life, you develop faith in the abundance and accessibility of resources, love, success, and happiness. When you let go of anxiety and scarcity to embrace thankfulness for what is already here, you allow yourself to be open to receiving abundance in many forms. *This optimistic anticipation starts an ever-evolving cycle of growth and fulfillment* as your behavior attracts peace and prosperity, which influences your behavior, which attracts even more peace and prosperity, and so on ...

Flow states are characterized by deep focus, heightened performance, and a sense of timelessness. I got your back on this one: Here are fourteen ways you can enter flow states and invite abundance into your life. We've touched on many of these; now, I'm putting it all together as a cheat sheet for the Effort Lens!

1. Passion and purpose fueled by patience. Engage in activities that genuinely excite and inspire you. When you're passionate about what you're doing, it's easier to enter a flow state, but here's a warning:

> I've always needed more patience in all of my life's most important areas. It's definitely a work in progress for me, but one thing I do understand is that *patience doesn't compromise ambition. Patience actually fuels the likelihood that you'll get the results you're looking for.* Knowing this inspires me to keep on practicing patience!
>
> Acting with ambition and patience can push you to play the game and strive for more without losing sleep or sacrificing your well-being. This is especially important for those of us with entrepreneurial DNA. It saddens me to see so many people who don't choose to balance their ambition with patience.
>
> If more of us truly understood that we have time, we'd realize that being patient and going at our own pace doesn't make us any less "driven." It makes us wise. Counterintuitively, patience speeds up

the process of naturally entering flow states and generating meaningful results in the most important areas of life because **we enter each effort with a clear mind and heart.**

2. Focus and presence. Practice mindfulness to enhance your ability to stay fully present in the moment. Minimize distractions and immerse yourself in the task at hand.

3. Positive mindset. Cultivate a positive attitude and believe in your ability to succeed, which will enhance your flow experiences.

> **Early in my studies in holistic health education,** I would laugh to myself at the people in class who would share their experience and invariably end it with a quick, "But I'm not going to beat myself up about it." Being really adept at beating myself up for all kinds of things, I couldn't believe people WEREN'T doing that. *Oh, is this one of those things you're supposed to say? Well, okay…*
>
> I soon learned that this was, in fact, an invitation to change, and I began practicing the inner voice process. Each small act of courage I noted (and negative messages I rejected) added up over time to a positive mindset. When you're in sales (and I've been in sales for a very long time), you face a lot of rejection. I'm grateful for my positive attitude and belief in my ability, both of which have

increased my capacity for rejection and enhanced my inner voice. And I am a lot kinder to myself.

4. Positive affirmations. Use positive affirmations—like the ones in Chapters One through Four—to reinforce your belief in abundance and your ability to experience it. Challenge limiting beliefs.

5. Clear goals. Set clear and achievable goals for your activities. Knowing what you want to accomplish provides a sense of direction and motivation.

> **One of the most audacious goals I set** when I started my company was important to me but not financially based: I would be able to walk or ride my bike to work every day as a form of environmental stewardship. Initially, I was driving nearly 50,000 miles a year to my clients' locations because much of my work required me to be physically present. By year four, I had built my network of trust-based relationships and alliances—and something else.
>
> I started to coach and train clients on, essentially, how to do parts of my job, such as taking measurements or developing the kind of design sketches I would make. Why didn't they ask, *Hey, why are we doing YOUR job?* Well, the payoff for them was that they became better warehouse operators and managers, and at times, they came up with better layouts than I could because they

were trained for it and knew their company best. I handed some power over to the customer, and we enjoyed a collaborative effort. Within four years, I was biking to work.

6. Skill development. Hone your skills and expertise in whatever you choose to put effort into. Mastery increases the likelihood of entering a flow state and keeps you within manageable expectations.

7. Self-challenge. Seek activities that are challenging but not overwhelming. Interesting point: Flow often occurs when you're in the zone between boredom and anxiety.

8. Feedback. Receive immediate feedback on your performance, which allows you to adjust and improve in real-time. Use your inner voice to give you objective, constructive feedback.

9. Time management. Allocate dedicated time for your chosen activities, allowing you to fully engage without worrying about external time constraints.

> **I was excited about starting my podcast** but concerned that the time requirement would adversely affect my work-life balance. Then, I looked at it through the lens of my values—following my passion, creating rather than consuming, and contributing to the community—and decided I would commit to being more adaptable in my schedule. The results have been amazing. I love hosting podcasts; I'm energized by it all. Yet, I had to be

willing to invite that change into my conception of time because it's the most precious thing we have. Turns out that when it comes to ROI (return on investment) on time spent, the podcast pays off not only as a business development tool, but as a personal development resource, passion project, and much more. I interviewed my dad a few months before he passed away. That's priceless.

10. Embracing challenge. View challenges as opportunities for growth rather than obstacles. Embracing difficulties instead of getting blocked by them keeps your flow state flowing.

11. Balance and self-care. Maintain a healthy work-life balance and prioritize self-care. Rest and relaxation are essential for entering flow states.

12. Variety. Mix up your routine by exploring new activities and experiences. Novelty can lead to increased flow states and a sense of abundance through diverse activities and perspective-enhancing experiences.

13. Gratitude. Practice gratitude daily to shift your focus to what you already have. A grateful mindset attracts more abundance into your life (helping you fill your abundance container).

14. Visualization. Visualize yourself in a flow state, fully engaged and excelling in your chosen activity (Think Coach Bob Morano and his visualization exercise with his football team). This mental rehearsal can enhance your ability to enter flow.

FOCUS ON PROCESS, NOT RESULTS

John Wooden created his own definition of success because Merriam-Webster's focus on "attainment of wealth, favor, or eminence" doesn't hold water. I'm with John.

> "Success is peace of mind, which is a direct result of self-satisfaction, knowing you made the effort to become the best you are capable of."
>
> —John Wooden, the greatest basketball coach of all time

Flow states toward creating abundance and success are highly individual experiences. What works for one person may not work for another. Experiment with different strategies and approaches to find what resonates best with you and consistently brings you into the flow state.

This concept was a big thing for me, particularly in building and running my business. In the last couple of years, I have developed an appreciation that **training and practice are key.** I can (and do!) have the greatest group of people in my company—smart, talented, hard-working, and with the best intentions. Yet the truth is that, because of their individual experiences, they don't always get what we want them to know the first time around. It takes a process of repetitive and experiential training, which never really ends as the business grows and changes.

A few years ago, I was too focused on results with my coaching (further encumbered by my lack of patience!), which had me frustrated when I didn't feel like the results I wanted were happening. I finally realized I wasn't investing the amount of time and money on the *process of training*. Now, I have a process. And as long as everyone involved commits to and advances that process (like John Wooden said), I'm focused on putting MY best foot forward and making the best effort I can. I'm surrendering to and flowing with it, getting better at it, and enjoying it—and apparently, so are my people.

Generally, in American society, we are too focused on results—financial worth, fame and celebrity are everything! Whatever we have to do to get to the top, we do it, only to find ourselves burned out and pissed off in the process. And the struggle can get even greater because we have to STAY ON TOP and can't fall off.

Remember Zack's quote from Chapter Five? *"No one on his deathbed ever said, 'I wish I had spent more time on my business."* The results they thought they wanted can end up taking over their lives.

The beauty of focusing on the process is that, as you expand and grow, you often find out that you didn't want that result you had been going for anyway—the new "result" is something better!

PAYOFF: BECOME AN AGENT OF CHILL

Jeremy, from the company I mentioned earlier called Rise 25, one day shared a line from a song called "Cruise," which he said reminded him of hanging out with me: "You make me wanna roll my windows down and cruise." I was flattered (and curious as to why *that* song...), and I assumed it was sincere because this particular guy knows I'll meet him at McDonald's and kick his ass if he's just messing with me. So, I dedicated this poem to him, which I wrote while working on this book.

Cultivate the Creative Force of Chill

When you discover who you truly are,
It's time to drive that fancy car.
Put your foot to the floor,
Free from worry anymore, because
YOU already know the final score.

Around 2nd or 3rd gear, you'll feel the flow;
Use it for much, much more than making dough
'Cause that would simply be the essence of a classy ho.'
Discover what you don't know you don't know;
Remember, you can't get upstream, no matter how hard you row.

Integrity will always trump celebrity;
Do what you say you'll do and
Avoid the people and practice of throwing poo.
Quietly stay the course of your will
By being completely still.

Cultivate the Creative Force of Chill.

HERE'S THE (INTER)CONNECTION

> "The worst teacher is one who thinks they have nothing left to learn."
>
> —Drake H.

Another aspect of acceptance, surrender and flow might seem unexpected: **coaching and being coached.** I believe that coaching is one of the most effective and rewarding practices you can have in business and life, and it's a huge part of my business strategy and approach. I see evidence all the time of how this practice generates value in our business ecosystem and separates us from our competitors. Within the organization, we coach each other, and we coach and get coaching from our clients, vendors, and strategic partners.

I'm not talking about finding a coach to hire or becoming a "certified" coach (as beneficial as that can be). I mean being receptive to learning from anyone who knows something you don't know. Look to the people you are interacting with on a day-to-day basis. How can you gain some knowledge, insight, or inspiration from their gifts?

Being willing to seek help is a strength, not a weakness. It can be hard to ask for help when you're a big shot like me :), but things become so much easier and better when I do.

I call out Rise 25 again (the company that produces my *Tao of Pizza* podcast) as a great example of some of the best coaching I've received. Rise 25 is not a coaching firm, yet, for me, every interaction with them is an opportunity to be coached. They've been an invaluable and generous resource for helping me outside the podcast space—how to find virtual assistants, do online meetings, prospect new clients, upgrade my scheduling apps, and many other ways to do business better.

My entire career has been supported by great "coaches" who surfaced in my network and shared their wisdom. In turn, I hope I've given helpful coaching. Some of the people I've coached have gone on to start multi-million-dollar companies of their own, so I might be on a roll!

WRAPPIN' IT UP

When I was young, I heard a speech given by a well-known business expert, Skip Ross, which had a profound effect on me. One of the recommendations he made on how to be a better businessperson was this: Read Scripture at least once a day. He said, "You have two options. If you believe in God, once a day is enough to read. If you don't believe in God, do it twice a day to get the same results."

I knew he was being a little bit tongue-in-cheek, and at the time, I thought it was funny, but I took the guy's word for it. I already knew about self-fulfilling prophecies and the lesson in Henry Ford's quote: "Whether you think you can, or you think you can't—you're right." So, it made sense to me.

I wasn't even sure what it meant to believe in God or not to believe, but the message I got that day led me on a path of self-discovery about the nature of ambition, effort, and flowing with the nature of life, not fighting against it or trying to one-up it.

At first, I definitely had to read things twice to get it, and it's been hard work sometimes, but it does get easier—it begins to flow and feels much more peaceful.

> "Life and love generate effort, but effort will not generate them. Faith in life, faith in other people and in oneself is the attitude of allowing the spontaneous to be spontaneous, in its own way and in its own time."
>
> —Alan Watts

GOING DEEPER

Think of the most audacious goals you have set for yourself. What is an area where you could use some help? There are many ways to coach and be coached. Find a mentor or hire a coach for a specific project. The process of going through what you're trying to accomplish can be beneficial by itself.

That's a powerful statement! Having audacious goals is one thing, but recognizing where you need help and actively seeking mentorship or coaching can make all the difference.

Finding the right coach or mentor starts with clarity on what you need help with. Identify the specific skills, knowledge, or experience you're looking for, whether it's career advancement, entrepreneurship, fitness, or personal growth. Start by tapping into your existing network—colleagues, industry events, and online communities like LinkedIn can be great places to find experienced professionals willing to mentor.

If you're looking for a more structured approach, consider hiring a certified coach through reputable organizations like the International Coach Federation (ICF) or exploring coaching platforms like BetterUp or Coach.me. Don't be afraid to reach out, ask questions, and have a trial conversation to ensure they're the right fit for your needs.

NOTES

INNERCHAPTER
MASTERY OF THE CREATIVE FORCE OF CHILL
(Mind-Body CrossFit)

The beauty of Bruce Lee's practice is that he colorfully blended a variety of martial arts training to create his own capital "A" art, called Jeet Kune Do. Lee also happened to create a fortune, unparalleled fame, and a cult following through this art. His concepts, quotes, and rebel style still inspire generations who didn't even grow up watching his movies, yet practice their moves on younger siblings two inches from the TV during commercials...

What do Bruce Lee, Werner Erhard, Napoleon Hill and Ken Wilber have in common? They all embody what I call "mixed martial arts for body, mind, and soul." Each of them created a path toward **mastery of the creative force of chill** through integrating practices that provide access to breakthrough performance and new revelations. Beautiful examples of creative Whole Person Paradigms.

When you're flowing with the creative force of chill, time becomes elastic, and the creative energy that arises is as dynamic, powerful, and ecstatic as the reality of life itself—**the power to imagine what is possible and to create it.**

"Everything is energy and that's all there is to it. Match the frequency of the reality you want, and you cannot help but get that reality. It can be no other way." —Attributed to Albert Einstein

Have some fun playing the long game, and try something on to expand your awareness. Don't be afraid to be like Bruce Lee, pulling from all kinds of sources and practices to create your own path (that's what this book is all about!). Being a curious amateur can be delightful when everybody can play the fool. Be curious about what you don't know you don't know.

THE FOUR PS OF PRACTICE:

#1: Posture. Rule number one of Jordan Peterson's *"12 Rules for Life: An Antidote to Chaos"* is: "Stand up straight with your shoulders back." Petersen supports his rule through research on lobsters, which showed that, when fighting for territory, the posture of the "winning" lobster influenced the behavior of the "defeated" lobsters such that their brain chemistry changed and they backed down. Posture influences your moods, personal energy, blood flow, self-image, and the reactions in your environment.

#2: Patience. Anyone who promises overnight results is usually full of it and trying to sell you something you don't need. Remember the lifelong learning marathon. However, like that fresh cup of water handed to you by the cheering bystander as you're running, you can experience early wins and breakthroughs that build some daily momentum. See the breakdowns, challenges, losses and setbacks for what they are—what life hands us to remind us that we are alive.

#3: Presence. Stay fully engaged in the present moment as much as you can. Be aware of the moods, emotions, and needs of others present as you share the energy space with a center for empathy and compassion. CHILL doesn't dwell on the past or project the future.

#4: Persistence. The most powerful creative force in the universe is love. When it comes to the practice of working with, generating, rejuvenating, and using energy as a creative force, I have found it useful in my practice to focus on the power of choosing to love. I mean love as a verb, not a "feeling" of love that comes and goes based on your moods or what's happening between your legs, but learning to *choose to love* regardless of the circumstances. Where does persistence come in? At least for me, choosing to love as a verb takes persistence. Maybe a lifelong practice. Don't laugh because it ain't as easy as Hollywood makes it look—but it's worth everything!

CHAPTER SEVEN

TUNING LENS—PERTINACITY

Fine-tune your awakening process

Now that I have you taking it easy (but taking it) like an Agent of Chill, I'm going to "nudge" you out of the nest. Never fear, here's a little preparation for the flight...

> "If you want to awaken all of humanity, then awaken ALL [emphasis mine] of yourself; if you want to eliminate the suffering in the world, then eliminate all that is negative in yourself. Truly, the greatest gift you have to give is that of your own self-transformation."
>
> —*Attributed to Lao Tzu*

Growth mindset. You have probably heard this term related to business. The conventional meaning, introduced to the world in the early aughts by renowned psychologist Carol Dweck, refers to individuals who want to strategically develop their talents for success or a company that supports their employees' ability to be more productive, collaborative, and empowered. All good for an individual to aspire to and practice in their professional life.

Now, let's blow it up and out for the Whole Person Paradigm: **A growth mindset is wanting to awaken ALL of yourself:**

- **To be aware of awareness.**
- **To fine-tune all the lenses: Spiritual, Emotional, Mental, and Action.**
- **To shift your six human gifts into gear and put your foot to the floor on mindful awareness, learning, and practices.**

About the route you will be taking? A growth mindset means creating your own path where there is no path. Moreover, you're never going to "arrive"—it's a *continuing journey on a path you've never known.* Each step you take is like your first, and with each step, you are not the same person you were before.

> "A path is made by walking on it."
>
> —Attributed to Chuang Tzu

Pertinacity. Million-dollar word, isn't it? Go ahead, impress everybody by slipping it into the conversation at your next get-together. The idea of pertinacity was introduced to me by the colleague I mentioned earlier, Bonnie Artman Fox, as a critical quality for leaders to have in order to build trust and be a positive influence. For me, it means **courage, conviction, and a little bit of stubbornness.** It's persistence and tenacity to stick with what's difficult. Pertinacity is a cousin of resilience, which is my favorite quality. You will need to develop pertinacity for the Tuning Lens journey.

Mindfulness: Is it Woo-Woo or Kick-ass?

> **I met with a prospective client who was interested in coaching** with me, and she started out with, "I have to be honest, I'm just really not that comfortable with what I call New Age BS." On the other end of the phone line, all the way across the country, I could almost see her narrow, steely scowl looking down her nose over the top of her horn-rimmed glasses.
>
> In truth, I get it. I'm a ravenous seeker of the unexplained mysteries of life—and I also cringe at some of the claims so frequently made in the realm of personal and professional growth. As my wife would say, "It sounds like a lot of "hokey pokey."
>
> But to me, it could also be, "THAT's what it's all about!" So, my life and practice are a **process of**

fine-tuning—seeing, tasting, and feeling what is and what is not.

Back to the story... I explained the value of holistic practices in personal and professional development. She asked, "Do you have research that supports that?" And, in fact, I did.

Even though I've found that mindfulness is one of the key practices needed to develop holistically, I was still shocked to learn how much research has been done on mindful practices. I can't tell you what a delight and a relief it was for me to be able to answer her question and point to specific resources where she could verify the value of holistic practices for herself.

In my research, I found this awesome graphic that tells it all:

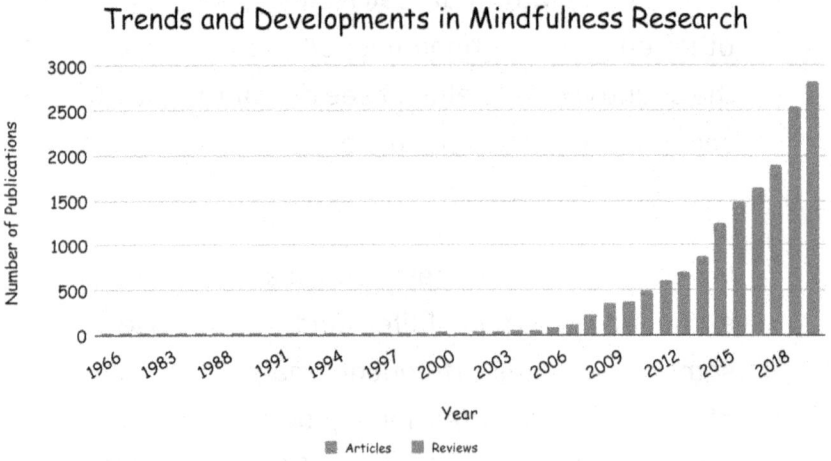

As for this potential client, as of this writing, I don't know whether or not she will do business with me. Either way, I was left with the impression that I introduced her to some new ways of seeing herself and her opportunities that she didn't have before. Even if we never speak again, that's an impact I can feel good about.

Maybe there are reasons why you, too, might want to be able to offer a rigorous, grounded, and credible response to this kind of genuine desire to understand things about your unique approach to business, personal, and family life. I hope this chart is a good start.

USING THE SIX GIFTS FOR THE TUNING LENS

It's probably no surprise that cultivating and fine-tuning your awareness is a cornerstone of the Whole Person Paradigm. Imagine life as a symphony, where you are both the conductor and the instrument.

Feeling overwhelmed by the demands of her career, Sarena decides to allocate time each day for mindfulness meditation. Her inner voice becomes her guiding melody. It whispers insights, encouraging her to cultivate mental clarity and emotional balance through deliberate practice. Sarena's inner voice helps her attune to the present moment and reconnect with her inner harmony. As a result, she naturally begins to radiate energy that is warm, inviting, and enlivening in all of her pursuits.

Choice is the conductor's baton, guiding the melody of our existence. Choice empowers us to select the harmonious notes that resonate with our inner essence. It's the beginning of alignment with our deepest values, setting the stage for a life in tune with our authentic selves.

Imagination writes the musical score of the future we are going to create. It allows us to envision a life aligned with our deepest aspirations. Through imagination and creativity, we craft a path that leads us to alignment with our purpose and passions.

Self-awareness is our tuning fork as we navigate life's complex symphony. It helps us recognize when we are in harmony or discord with ourselves and the world. Through self-awareness, we adjust our actions and choices to fine-tune our attunement.

Sensation of the six senses grounds us in the wisdom of our bodies. It allows us to perceive subtle physical sensations that signify alignment or misalignment that may throw us off-key. We make choices that promote physical and emotional well-being by listening to these cues.

Humor, our playful accompanist, infuses joy and laughter in our attunement journey, reminding us not to take ourselves too seriously. It lightens the weight of self-improvement, boosts our resolve, and makes the path more enjoyable.

I like to think of attunement as if we humans are an instrument, and we tune our instrument for all the different things we can do in this life. We can touch people's lives, inspire creativity, create solutions, optimize our worldview more holistically to expand our vision of what the future could look like, and take meaningful action toward our full potential!

SIX ASPECTS OF THE TRANSFORMATIVE POWER OF MINDFULNESS: UNLEARNING AND LEARNING

Right, I hear ya... We have spent our whole young lives in a society that puts a premium on learning. It's drilled into us as adults, and I'm going to ask you to UNlearn. It's not my fault—blame these folks:

Zen Buddhism emphasizes the importance of letting go of preconceived notions and habitual thinking patterns. The process often involves UNlearning what one thinks as one approaches life with a "beginner's mind" (*shoshin*).

Taoism advocates for simplicity and returning to a state of naturalness. The principle of *wu wei* (non-action or effortless action) involves UNlearning artificial behaviors and social conditioning to align more closely with the Tao (The Way).

Advaita Vedanta is a Hindu philosophical tradition in which UNlearning is related to the process of *Neti-Neti* (not this, not that). Practitioners are encouraged to strip away all layers of false identification and ignorance to realize the true self, Brahman (the ultimate reality).

Sufism, in Islamic mysticism, engages Sufis in practices aimed at shedding the ego and worldly attachments to attain a state of union with the Divine. This often involves UNlearning the illusions of the self and the material world.

Christian Mysticism shares many of the same principles as the spiritual traditions listed above. At its heart, the goal is to transcend ego-driven desires of the world and to serve others selflessly.

So, we're standing on some mighty shoulders here! The journey of mindfulness is a profound one of **UNlearning and learning, which enables you to unlock your mind's full potential.** You are delving into the intricacies of the subconscious, identifying patterns, transcending knee-jerk reactions, exploring blind spots, and embracing the mind-body connection.

When you cultivate these skills, you stand to exponentially increase focus, awareness, and overall effectiveness in both personal and professional realms! Let's dive into the six aspects...

#1: Power of the subconscious. The assertion that 80% or more of the mind is subconscious underscores the significance of exploring this vast and often uncharted territory.

#2: Patterns and repairs. Mindfulness invites a keen observation of patterns—both thought and behavior. You get to repair or replace patterns that hinder your personal and professional growth. As we're fine-tuning our awakening process, let's stretch our perspective on patterns.

The amazing Greg Bateman, author of *Steps to an Ecology of Mind: Collected Essays in Anthropology, Psychiatry, Evolution, and Epistemology,* challenges us with this question: "What pattern connects the crab to the lobster and the orchid to the primrose and all four of them to me? And me to you?"

Bateson argues that the environmental crisis is mainly the result of an imaginative failure on the part of humans to correctly see how they're connected to the broader web of life. He believes we should think and feel beyond our narrowly defined concepts of sustainability and suggests a new kind of architectural knowledge based on a study of the spaces we live in and how we can be connected to nature through them.

"You decide that you want to get rid of the by-products of human life and that Lake Erie will be a good place to put them. You forget that the eco-mental system called Lake Erie is a part of your wider eco-mental system—and that if Lake Erie is driven insane, its insanity is incorporated in the larger system of your thought and experience."

Playing with the patterns of life as you know them and scrutinizing them allows you to break free of unhelpful repetitive cycles and inspire adaptability and innovation. Repairing patterns is an essential step in the UNlearning process to **integrate new and beneficial ways of thinking and acting**.

#3: Transcending knee-jerk reactions. Mindfulness practices empower you to transcend knee-jerk reactions, enabling a more thoughtful and measured response to stimuli. In the business and personal realms, knee-jerk reactions can lead to impulsive decisions or responses that may not align with long-term goals. ***Through mindfulness, you gain the ability to pause, reflect, and respond with intention, which heightens your sense of control and focus*** and opens you up to more expansive thinking and decision-making.

> **"ROMO" is usually related to pandemic loneliness** or avoiding the internet, but it has a different meaning for me. Being ROMO refers to Tony Romo, star quarterback of the Dallas Cowboys for fourteen seasons with an incredible record, YET never won a Super Bowl. That was his "failure," and he was trashed by fans and the press for it.
>
> Now, I have no idea if he had a mindfulness or any other personal growth practice. Tony deserves an acronym in my book because he stepped down from his starting quarterback position with grace and class. Instead of knee-jerk reactions with anger or blame or letting the opinions of others get to him, Romo gave an unforgettable press conference that showed he's no failure but a first-class success in every way. In it, he referred to two battles: ***"I feel like we all have two battles...one with the man across from you, the second is with the man inside of you... Once you control***

the one inside of you, the one across from you doesn't really matter."

I appreciate this man's guts to say, "I've put everything on the line to try and accomplish my goal... and worked hard to recover from those injuries to return to battle for myself, teammates and fans again and again. And now I have to humbly step aside and watch someone else do it instead. I am still proud, happy for my successor and teammates, and I am at peace with myself because I know I laid it ALL on the line."

#4: Blind-spot treasure hunt. Addressing blind spots is a critical aspect of mindfulness and a major contributor to increased awareness. By embarking on a "treasure hunt" for blind spots, you uncover hidden biases, assumptions, and perspectives that may have obstructed your growth. Then, you can make a choice whether to hold onto them or change them (thereby creating new and better patterns!). *Intentional exploration of blind spots enhances self-awareness, broadens your perspective, and opens up a more inclusive, compassionate outlook.*

Ask yourself:

"Am I making the pertinacious effort to be honest about my worldview?"
"Are there opportunities or possibilities I'm missing out on because of a certain way I'm thinking or believing?"

After interviewing my dad on my *Tao of Pizza* podcast, I asked him (with the recording still on for posterity), "Can you hang around for a little longer? I want to ask you one more question."

I asked him to share about his dad, my grandpa, who died before I was born. The truth is that I had NEVER asked him before because I never wanted to bring up that pain. As a kid, I made up a story that I recounted to myself over the years and had come to accept as true—my dad was young when his father died, and they weren't that close. Man, was I wrong!

Dad told me they were super close. My grandpa was my dad's hero. He coached in every Little League game, attended every school event, was a Boy Scout leader, and taught my dad so much.

To my surprise, he also said Grandpa was kind of a racist. "It was okay for us to have Mexican friends. I had a lot because we all grew up together in the Central Valley." He continued, "But my dad wouldn't allow my sisters to date Latino men. Then, his own niece married a Latino, and they had a son. Dad wanted to have a relationship with his niece and nephew, and if that was going to happen, he had to change his perspective. So, he did, and they enjoyed many good years together."

Then, the conversation turned emotional. Dad told me that when he was in college in Berkeley, his mom called late one night to say his father had had a massive heart attack and was in the ICU. My dad left campus in the middle of the night to drive to the hospital. I cannot imagine what he must have been thinking on the hour-and-a-half drive to Woodland. Once he got there, it was too late—he never got the chance to say goodbye to his father.

I felt so much compassion for my dad in that moment, more than I ever thought possible, and we just sat quietly for a long time. It was an amazing bonding moment.

The compassion for my dad generated a physical change in my body. My six senses were all tingling. I thought about my kids, who were about the same age as he had been, one of them far away at college. What if it happened to them? It's impossible to explain how much closer I felt to my dad.

He passed away three weeks later.

I can honestly say that if I hadn't been doing mindfulness practices over these years, I would have carried my false story to my grave. What a lot of time I wasted by not asking—and I almost lost my chance to ever know the truth! This blind spot had prevented me from being aware of something so important in my life, and in my dad's life, as well.

Another blind-spot lesson: My grandpa's blind spot about people he thought were different from himself. When I first heard this, I felt somewhat ashamed of him, but then I realized how much courage it must have taken for him to open his mind to something different. Now, I feel proud that somebody in my family made such a monumental shift in perception because I know people who have not done so, and their children carry the same racism into their adult lives ... so the legacy continues.

When it comes to my own worldview, I look for opportunities that I might be missing because I have a particular belief about the way things are and the way certain things are going to be and "should be." It is humbling, and I am grateful for this lesson.

#5: Noticing physical sensations. Mindfulness extends beyond mental awareness to incorporate the physical realm. The practice encourages you to notice what it physically feels like when you engage in various thoughts or activities. *This heightened awareness of physical sensations serves as an anchor, grounding you in the present moment.* By recognizing the mind-body connection, you can better navigate stressors, enhance resilience and pertinacity, and channel your energy toward focused and effective endeavors.

#6: Know self to no-self continuum. The journey from knowing oneself to embracing the no-self continuum signifies a deepening of mindfulness practice. *As you peel away layers of socially conditioned thinking and ego-driven responses, you move closer to a state of pure awareness.*

These six aspects of mindfulness synergistically combine to increase focus, awareness, and effectiveness—exponentially! You can see that bringing in pertinacity CAN change your life. As you UNlearn limiting beliefs, you:

- Integrate new perspectives that help you navigate the complexities of life with more intention and clarity.
- Feel more empathy and compassion in your everyday life.
- Experience a more profound connection with yourself and with the external world, allowing a heightened understanding of your sense of purpose and meaning.

And that's just the inside! Turning outward, you find yourself equipped to face challenges with resilience, make informed decisions, and cultivate a more balanced and purposeful existence.

What's not to love?!

THE PAYOFF: EVERYONE'S DOING THE TRANSCENDANCE

As I was writing this book, I kept making the same spelling error—*transcendAnce* instead of *transcendEnce*. Even though I knew the correct spelling, I messed it up every time. Frustrated, I tried to figure out why, and BINGO—a transcendent realization! It IS a dance!

Our journey progresses from knowing ourselves to embracing the no-self continuum—a transcendent state where the ego dissolves and a profound sense of interconnectedness emerges.

This stage of the metaphorical surf parallels the ride: the pinnacle of the surfing experience. If you've ever surfed, you know what I'm talking about. Or if you have ever felt that sublime rush at a peak moment of performance or achievement. Likewise, in life, **the cultivation of awareness leads to a state of stoke, where we find joy and fulfillment in the ride**, even amid the inevitable challenges.

Where does transcenDANCE come in? Fine-tuning awareness is an intricate **dance between effort and surrender** as we mindfully move through life with grace and purpose. Like the surfer seeking the perfect wave, we attune to our inner currents to find a sense of stoke—a joy that arises from our professional and personal experiences that is nothing short of a transcenDANCE!

> "The only way to make sense out of change is to plunge into it, move with it, and join the dance."
>
> —*Alan Watts*

Doing the TranscenDANCE is all well and good when the waves of life are predictable and the weather's sunny. What about those other times when there's conflict, for example, between you and someone else? How do you navigate when discord happens in your world?

Here's a handy tip: Before you say another word or react defensively, P.A.U.S.E.

>**P**ause: Take a beat by focusing on your breath to stay anchored in the present moment.

Allow: Bring awareness to what's happening inside of you, in your body. Identify what you're feeling.

Understand: The fight-or-flight reaction is getting triggered in both of you, which is understandable, given the nature of the conversation or situation. Still, you are in charge of managing YOUR reaction. Find that place of understanding where you are in this moment.

Sink In: Let calmness sink in as you continue to breathe, putting the brakes on your fight-or-flight reaction and allowing rational thinking to surface. And remember to ...

Emotionally un-charge: Even though the other person may act defensively and emotionally, you can calm your internal environment and take the charge out of your own emotions. Doing so will have a positive impact on that person and the others around you in that moment.

HERE'S THE (INTER)CONNECTION: CATCH THE WAVE

Diving deeper into the surfing world-as-life, I turn to Srinivas Rao in his book *Unmistakable: Why Only Is Better Than Best* and his sexy surfing metaphor for creating an unmistakable life, to help me illustrate the art of fine-tuning awareness.

In the vast ocean of life, challenges ebb and flow like the waves. In the last chapter, we focused on effortless effort, dedicating time and energy to navigate and BE in harmony with the intricate currents of life. "Making it look easy" is the paddle out—when the surfer moves out into the ocean on their board to get into the best position to catch a wave—the foundational stage where we must meet the challenges and uncertainties of the journey. We become **conscious of the unconscious.** It looks easy when you're watching them, but it takes a lot of practice, dedication and training to paddle out.

Now, we go deeper into the consistent effort required to cultivate a heightened state of awareness. Mastery demands intentional and sustained effort, whether in surfing or in life. Srini Rao insightfully brought those parallels to life in my podcast interview with him.

As the process unfolds, the focus is on the "lineup"—the area where the waves are breaking—and surfers are now on their boards, sitting and waiting for the perfect set. Surfing has a rule that establishes order and safety in the lineup, relating to who has the right-of-way to surf a particular wave. Think of the Golden Rule: If someone is up and riding on a wave, you don't attempt to paddle for it. I take Srini's metaphor of the "drop" in surfing to mean the idea of navigating the waves in life—the inevitable space where challenges and opportunities demand deliberate, measured responses. When is it your time? When is it your lane?

Patience, flow, and timing; eventually, your opportunities come. It's where the cultivation of awareness begins, where we learn to read the subtle cues of life's waves. The skilled surfer identifies the optimal part of the wave to prepare for their next move. In our practice, we observe the **patterns and repairs**—what is governing our thoughts, behaviors, and reactions—and discern which patterns contribute to our personal and professional growth. What's our next, best move, and who do we need to BE to make it?

And then comes the do-or-die moment—action. You won't catch any waves sitting on the beach or in your recliner! The "impact zone" is the area where a wave breaks and its force is the most concentrated. Surfers need to be aware of the impact zone to avoid being caught in the crashing waves. It's the inevitable consequence of the adventure of life—fine-tuning awareness and practice as you move through the impact zones of life—cultivating the path, the ride, and "stoke," the reason we surf in the first place! In the ride of life, the stoke is realizing how far you've come in your training and the incredible power of being able to "catch a wave."

In life, we fine-tune our awareness to **rise above knee-jerk reactions** to stimuli. Through mindfulness and self-reflection, we conceive a more intentional and focused approach to the myriad situations we may encounter—what impact they will have on us, and the impact we may have on others.

Surfing is a mental game that includes relentless hours of training, managing fear, understanding risk, and calling up courage. For us, the **blind-spot treasure hunt** lets us explore the uncharted territories within ourselves. Unearthing biases, assumptions, and perspectives that might be obstructing our growth becomes a transformative exercise. Areas that need our careful attention are illuminated, guiding us toward a more comprehensive and nuanced understanding of our mental landscape.

Just as the surfer tunes into the subtle movements of the ocean and wind conditions in search of the perfect wave, we **notice our physical sensations** to gain a deeper understanding of our emotional and mental states. We emphasize the mind-body connection as a conduit to heightened awareness. This awareness serves as an important guide, allowing us to navigate the complexities of life with greater resilience and balance.

And remember the most important lesson about surfing: The ocean always wins, so go with the flow!

WRAPPIN' IT UP

You might wonder why I didn't go into specific mindfulness practices and how-tos in this chapter. Well, meditation and the transcenDANCE can be dicey things to "teach." As you know by now (I hope), I want you to carve out YOUR OWN path to peace and prosperity. Thus, I am not here to dictate any specific way of cultivating your Tuning Lens.

Cheer up—I won't leave you completely alone by throwing you off the cliff without a parachute!

The goal is to **find a comfortableness in your practice.** Try them on for size—not too tight, not too itchy. The insights, experience, and guidance I'm sharing are mine in all their perfect imperfection, hoping to give you a framework to find practices that will help you live in more awareness and to awaken your whole self, *in your own way and on your own terms.*

Two final thoughts on attunement:

Scrap the idea that you will ever "arrive." The attunement process is just something you'll always go through—it has lifelong learner value.

The other thing is not to take it all too seriously (exercise that humor muscle!). If you find you are getting too much into the practice of attunement and trying to be an expert, then you're not doing the right thing. Just go *ROMO*, invite awakening, integrate what you learn, and put to use whatever you know in the moment.

GOING DEEPER

Choose a practice that intrigues you and try it on for 7-21 days. Write your thoughts about it and notice any effects the practice might be having. You may not notice anything at first, which means either you need to try it out longer (if you're enjoying it) or try out a different practice—it's YOURS TO CHOOSE!

Write down a commitment to yourself to continue to practice and stick to it. Something as simple as 2-7 minutes a day can make an exponential difference over time. Maybe it's something from this book or our website, something you find on the interwebs, taking guitar lessons, taking a walk every day—just make something up. And the more you do it, the better you'll get at it. The key is to simply Be, as a practice.

NOTES

INNERCHAPTER
THE PRINCE AND THE SHARPEST KNIFE

There was once a butcher who worked for Prince Wen Hui. He had worked there for many years and was unsurpassed in his ability to cut up an ox without ever sharpening his knife, which maintained its original razor-sharp edge over many years.

The butcher would move his shoulder just so, and the meat would fall away from the bone so easily, so smoothly. Again, swish, swish… He moved his cleaver smoothly and rhythmically. It was as though he were conducting a fantastic symphony—and all the while, meat simply fell away from the bone.

Prince Wen was entranced and one day asked the butcher how he had arrived at such mastery. The butcher laid down his cleaver and looked at the prince. "It is simple, my Lord. I am a follower of the Way (Tao) in everything I do. When I first began to cut up an ox, all I could see was the part of the ox in front of me. It took me three long years before I was able to see the entire ox in one glance.

"I no longer see it with my eyes but with my spirit. In this way, I am able to let the knife itself follow the grain of the meat on its own. I let the knife slice its own way through the hollows of the ox, never touching the tendons or ligaments, much less the bone.

"By following the Natural Way and letting the knife do the work, I have become a Master Butcher. A good cook cuts forcefully through the meat and must sharpen his knife every year. A mediocre cook hacks and chops at the meat and must sharpen his knife every month. My knife, on the other hand, has not been sharpened since I began using it nineteen years ago. And it is as sharp as the day I first took it up.

"There are spaces in the ox that the thin blade can cut through as if through air. There is plenty of space there for the blade to enter and move freely. This is why my blade is still so sharp after cutting up thousands of oxen.

"Sometimes, I come upon a difficult cut. Instead of wielding my blade harder, I stop completely and meditate upon the situation. I look very closely at the joint and move my blade very, very slowly, using no force, until suddenly, plop, the meat falls away like a clump of earth falling to the ground. Then, I stop and look around me to see if I am still in accord with the Way. If I am, then I am happy. I wipe my blade very carefully and put it away. Finished."

INSIDE THE PARABLE OF THE OX BUTCHER

First, the story reveals the three stages of development on the Taoist path: seeing the parts, seeing the whole, and seeing with spirit or energy (which you remember from way back in *Chapter*

One). It is also a vivid example of the Taoist concept of *effortless action* (wu-wei).

Sometimes, in order to move through difficult obstacles in our lives, we could be more effective by applying this principle of no force. Then, just like the meat falls away from the bone for the master cook, our own obstacles fall away before us so that we are able to see the whole and BE the Way.

The story also tells us that this practice can take some time to cultivate. It took the cook three long years before he was able to look at an ox, not with his eyes but with his spirit or energy. Anything of great value can take a long time of practice and cultivation to attain. It is impossible to gain mastery in a weekend seminar or by simply reading a book on mindfulness (even this one!).

Several years of practice leads to self-cultivation, and continual practice *is* the Way.

Was the story about an actual cook masterfully cutting up an actual ox? Stories, myths and metaphors are such powerful ways of learning new concepts. I love this story, and I am reminded of it every time I carve up a piece of meat. I think about the art of mastery and wonder why I sometimes have to hack and chop when serving others.

CHAPTER EIGHT

CIRCULAR CYCLICAL LENS—PROCESS

Expand the edges of the container of consciousness

Full disclosure: I'm a designer and have a Type-A personality. I have a lingering attachment to models and constructs, so this chapter was particularly challenging to write. There are models that dictate how people should dress or appear in public, or how businesses should be run, or processes planned—all offering useful frameworks for personal and professional development.

Over the years, I've found myself wrestling with a drive to master these models—and discovered I was missing the deeper point entirely. If you recall my story about the devout lady in the 1870s who was stuck in her own beliefs, you'll get that I needed to bring out the metaphorical Windex and wipe clean my Spiritual Lens!

So, why don't you and I work together to transcend limiting models and constructs right now?

Hell, we're going to shatter them, blow them up! Not out of whimsy but to explore our attachments to them. To what purpose? To challenge the confines of our consciousness, to break free from limiting models, and to embrace the infinite possibilities of the unknown. It's about *transcending boundaries and opening ourselves to the vastness of human potential.*

In a word: **Freedom.**

So, buckle up and start your engine!

THE POWER OF CREATIVE DESTRUCTION

It was tough for me to put the idea of the Whole Person Paradigm into words until I hit up Bucky Fuller's tetrahedron to help me frame the concept in a way that generates a three-dimensional representation of human potential. The THPM was my attempt to understand the interrelationships of multidimensional concepts like the four "faces" of mind, body, spirit, and emotion, and the six "edges" of self-awareness: imagination, inner voice, choice, sensations of the six senses, and humor. And you made a pretty little model of it for your own enjoyment and insight.

Now, I'm going to blow it all up!

What?? Why did I make you work on the damn thing?

Well, we humans need models and constructs to live civilly with each other and to understand ideas that are complex and even unmeasurable. Constructs can be useful. At the same time, they can be limiting, or we outgrow them as we get new information and a more enlightened understanding.

Think about growing up believing that 2+2=4, then finding out that 2+2 ALSO equals 6! Talk about pulling the reality rug right out from under you! Either way, the math is still a mental construct limited to explaining a two-dimensional world. And the tetrahedral model is an awesome, yet limited, construct to represent the three-dimensional world.

Here's the money point: **Even the best models and constructs can confine our ability to expand our consciousness and embrace the vast field of potential and possibility.** Some hold us in a narrow, constrained space to the point where we are limiting our everyday life—and we are not even aware that it's happening.

So, how do you learn, understand, and LIVE to your full human potential—as a Whole Person?

BUSTING OUT OF THE CONTAINER OF CONSCIOUSNESS

In the vast expanse of consciousness lies uncharted territory, ripe with potential and possibility. Within this realm, we find ourselves confronted with the ever-present cycles of life, death and rebirth—fundamental forces that shape our existence in ways both seen and unseen, some understood and some beyond our imagination.

In the course of this journey, we encounter the remnants of past constructs and models that have guided our understanding of the world. **These familiar structures have given us a sense of safety and security—up to a point.**

As we open up our view of life through our various lenses, we sense a discontent beneath the veneer of stability.

We chafe against the limitations of our models, sensing there is *more to life than what they prescribe.*

Like a caged bird yearning for the open sky, our spirits cry out for liberation from the confines of our own making.

You're feeling it, aren't you? That's why you're still with me ...

We begin to recognize that even the most appealing models can become constraints on our potential, particularly our collective potential. **Breaking free from those models offers a newfound freedom, one that surpasses the confines of the models themselves.**

With the awareness and tools we've been working with so far, we are now doing nothing less than embracing the cycles of life, death, and rebirth! We are accepting the ceaseless changes of it all. We are being fully present to and accepting what "is." We are open to "BEing" what is necessary, what is possible, and what is impossible for the future.

We are looking out from our safe, confined containers to the BIGGEST picture in order to:

> break through
>
>> let go of our attachments
>>
>>> build back up a new, freer, more awakened and meaningful life.

In this moment of reckoning, we can choose to cling to the familiar comforts of our constructs—or take on uncertainty into uncharted territory.

> "The Edge ... There is no honest way to explain it because the only people who really know where it is are the ones who have gone over... But the edge is still Out there."
>
> —Hunter S. Thompson

When was the last time you went over the Edge—that space where you crossed a threshold and things got a little warped, disrupted? Everyone has their own breakthrough experiences that transcend limits and barriers that were once powerful, and then—Poof! They vanish. As Thompson said, there really is no way to explain it, perhaps because people who haven't shared similar experiences would label "us" crazy. Yet how can we explain our experiences when we're using the language of the constructs and models we are used to, and they aren't cutting it anymore?

If you're one of these people, be heartened! In the annals of human history, there exist tales of individuals who have dared to defy convention and break free from the shackles of their conditioning. From the mystics of ancient civilizations to the visionaries of modern times, these trailblazers have charted a course beyond the boundaries of conventional wisdom and accepted constructs. They have forged a path of self-discovery and enlightenment, their stories illuminating the way forward for us.

One such figure is Saint Francis of Assisi—yes, the guy represented as a garden statue, an embodiment of peace and serenity, gently holding birds and animals in his arms. There's more than meets the eye to that iconic image. Born into wealth and status in the late 12th century, Frances di Pietro di Bernardone was a party animal! He was witty and handsome, full of high spirits and mischief. His partying buddies dubbed him "Dominus," the King of Parties, because he would throw lavish revelries with food, wine, and women.

He had always dreamed of being a warrior and fought in the war between Assisi and Perugia. He was captured and imprisoned for nearly a year, where he fell seriously ill and experienced what he believed were visions of God. In 1203, he was on his way to enlist in the army of Walter III when he had a vision from God (which he later recounted), who told him to turn around and go home—that he was meant for other things. And so, he did.

Upon returning to his village, Francis encountered a leper, considered a dangerous outcast by their culture. Fear and revulsion gripped the young man at the sight of the sick man in his path. Then, a transformational moment of grace occurred. He realized he feared the leper more than facing frontline action in a brutal war, which felt very wrong. Francis dismounted his horse and warmly embraced and tenderly kissed the leper.

In his testament, Francis would write: "When I was in sin, the sight of lepers nauseated me beyond measure; but then God himself led me into their company, and I had pity on them. When I had become acquainted with them, what had previously nauseated me became a source of physical consolation."

After this "encounter" with the Holy Spirit, Francis renounced his former life of wealth and privilege to dedicate himself to a spiritual path of serving all of God's creatures, including the sick, poor, outcasts, and animals. He went on to found the Franciscan Order, which became known for its emphasis on poverty, humility, and care for the marginalized, and still exists today. He was canonized as a saint by the Catholic Church after his death in 1226, forever known as Saint Francis of Assisi.

What a great reminder of the transformative power of breaking free from the constraints of our own making! St. Francis was a person who found a **freedom that transcended material possessions—a freedom rooted in the boundless expanse of human consciousness.**

Just to be clear, I'm not suggesting you renounce everything and go full-blown dedication to poverty and service (I think you can guess that I'm not doing that!). This is just one way to expand one's edges of consciousness—and it makes a great story, right?

You might also have noticed that St. Francis didn't suddenly have a huge epiphany in one miraculous earth-shattering moment that changed everything forever (one thing I left out of the story is that after his visions while sitting ill in the prison cell, he promptly went home to continue his partying life...). The fact is that **transformation is not a one-time event; it's a continual process of growth and evolution.** We all have our own little and large versions of Hunter Thompson's "Edges" out there as we confront the myriad attachments and limitations that bind us in our quest for life as a Whole Person.

Our interior experiences hold immense significance, even if they can't be fully captured by external measures and models. Like St. Francis, facing his fear of lepers, we have our own fears and attachments to confront that will pave the way to spiritual growth. When we choose to examine our attachment to the models, norms and perceptions that don't serve us anymore, we bust out of our confining containers and embrace the light of self-awareness.

THE JOURNEY OF LIBERATION

> "Tell me, what do you plan to do with your one wild and precious life?"
>
> —Poet Mary Oliver

Mary Oliver's question is where we find the essence of liberation, rooted in the boundless expanse of human consciousness. Mary Oliver challenges us not just to survive but to take advantage of our one wild and precious life in all its limitlessness!

So, let's embrace the infinite possibilities of existence and hop on the journey of self-discovery and transformation to find **the true essence of our being—a being that is infinite, eternal, and free.**

Caution! Potential roadblock ahead: There can be a sinking feeling that settles in when we contemplate letting go of these models to which we've paid homage all our lives, maybe even for generations. They've been an anchor for us, yet we know that, ultimately, they are flimsy and not dependable.

Remember all the way back to *Chapter One,* when we talked about how faith is an intrinsic hope ready for you to use to make a difference? I quoted the Apostle Paul, who wrote, "We walk by faith, not sight." In these moments, you call up your faith that the journey will be worth it! You remember that caged bird who wants to break through the bars and soar to freedom. You view the path through your four Lenses and employ the six human gifts—self-awareness, imagination, inner voice, choice, sensations of the six senses, and humor—to expand your consciousness, navigate the ebbs and flows, and make sound choices that will take you forward.

The journey to liberation is not linear. It is a dance of light and shadow, joy and sorrow, birth and death. In embracing life's cycles, you find the courage to let go of your attachments and understand the flow of existence. In accepting life's impermanence, you see the freedom to live fully in the present moment—and celebrate each one!

The journey to liberation is not without its challenges. As you venture into the unknown, you are confronted with the shadows that lurk within you—the fears, doubts, and insecurities that threaten to derail your progress. In these moments of darkness, you can listen to your inner voice for discernment and summon the light of self-awareness to help you work with the conditioning that has shaped your perceptions of reality. Whether cultural norms dictate your behavior or personal traumas inform your choices, you examine the roots of your conditioning and free yourself from their grip.

You tap into imagination, choice and humor to cultivate the courage to act on your insights, step boldly into the unknown, and welcome the infinite possibilities of existence. **With each act of courage, you draw closer to embracing the wholeness of your everyday life and of existence itself.**

The journey to liberation is not a solitary one. It is a collective endeavor that calls you to reach beyond your own boundaries and embrace the interconnectedness of all life. You'll remember

I mentioned Michael Murphy, co-author of *God and the Evolving Universe: The Next Step in Personal Evolution*. Well, his incredible story continues...

In 1950, Stanford pre-med student Michael Murphy stumbled upon Prof. Frederic Spiegelberg's course in Eastern philosophy and religion, and completely changed his trajectory.

He left the pre-med program to study the intersection of Eastern and Western thought beyond the conventional boundaries of Western education toward a more holistic view of human potential. Seeking a deeper understanding of these ideas, Michael spent an immersive year living and studying at an ashram in India, and returned to the U.S. convinced that true insight into human consciousness meant combining the strengths of both traditions. This journey led him to co-founding the Esalen Institute in California in 1962 (xx) and becoming a pioneer in the integral exploration of human consciousness, potential, and transformative possibilities.

"The internal world is the last frontier," Murphy says, "We all know about exploring outer space, but the human race is not fully acquainted with the stupendous nature of this inner frontier. We have no idea of our limits."

From my experience, the simplest way I can explain the interconnectedness of life is this: **We are all a drop in the ocean and the entire ocean in a drop—this is our inherent unity.** One drop isn't better or worse than any other, and we all flow together in our own ways, playing our particular roles, to form the vast body of water that supports life and the earth's existence.

Michael Murphy has enjoyed a front-row seat at the Human Potential Movement longer than I've been here on this planet. The Integral Life podcast did a three-part interview with him a few years ago, in which he was asked what he thought was the most important thing behind the success of the Esalen Institute. His answer was twofold. First, they hosted a wide variety of practitioners from many different perspectives, and second, nobody played "Capture the Flag," meaning no one particular modality claimed to be the winner, magic pill, or silver bullet.

LET'S CHOOSE NOT TO PLAY CAPTURE THE FLAG

We are fortunate to be accompanied by the wisdom of those who have gone before us—sages, saints, and mystics (like the ones you're finding in this book) who have charted a course beyond the confines of conventional wisdom. Their teachings serve as guideposts to illuminate the way forward.

We also learn from each other how to let go of old paradigms and perspectives. Through people and situations I've encountered along my own journey to liberation, there are parts of me that have died (thank God ...).

Ron Mikus was a close friend and business associate who encouraged, mentored, and supported me in my early business endeavors. He was a cocky, boisterous character with a sailor's mouth and a hot temper. Ron had a close relationship with a business mogul I wanted to connect with, named Sal. One day, I heard Ron talking about what I thought was a business event hosted by this individual. I wanted in!

I bugged Ron until he said to me, laughing, "Listen, Hiddleson, you're kind of an asshole." I replied with, "So are you! And you're best friends with this guy!" He instead invited me to another event. "We attend this jazz festival every year on Catalina Island. If you come to that, you'll get an introduction to Sal and maybe be invited to other events where top leaders and innovators in our business hang out to socialize and share ideas."

Although I couldn't care less about jazz, I was committed 100%! I was going to drag my family to this thing, hell or high water, because I thought knowing this guy would be a big break for my company. That was my mindset and motivation as I set out to impress (grumbling most of the way about the jazz part). I even rented a helicopter to make dinner on time!

Well, imagine my surprise to discover we were having a great time! I came to love jazz, and Sal and I became close friends. He is a fifty-year industry veteran and a Who's Who in the engineering community in our industry. He's become like a father, uncle, and mentor to me over the years. It was Sal who called me when Ron passed away and asked me to speak at his celebration of life. He's been a guest on my podcast, and our families remain close.

I'm still embarrassed to admit my unscrupulous motivation to meet him in the first place, but it's worth it to "out" myself for the sake of a good example of waking up to a new reality that brought joy and connection in a whole new way.

The "old vision" of business-building through networking relationships had to die in order to generate space for a new vision—the value of meaningful relationships as a tool to expand the possibilities to experience more of the life I've been given (more on the limitless power of relationships in the next chapter).

Take advantage of what you encounter in the course of the day to observe a perception or construct that isn't real or true for you anymore. Learn from the people around you about their ways of thinking. You never know what will come up.

THE PARADOX OF ATTACHMENT AND DETACHMENT

In the quest for liberation, we encounter the paradox of attachment and detachment. On one hand, we are called to release our grip on the familiar comforts of our constructs, relinquishing the false sense of security they provide. On the other hand, an invitation beckons us to embrace the richness of human experience in all its complexity, allowing us to be fully present to the joys and sorrows of life.

Through this process of surrender, we open ourselves to the infinite possibilities of consciousness. Like a river flowing freely to the sea, we are carried along by the currents of existence (remember our surfer friend, Srini Rao), buoyed by the knowledge that we are part of something greater than ourselves. This is where the ideas of surrender and flow take their starring role. In this state of surrender, **we find a peace that surpasses understanding—a peace rooted in the boundless expanse of human consciousness.**

> "We seldom realize...that our most private thoughts and emotions are not actually our own. For we think in terms of languages which we did not invent, but which were given to us by our society."
>
> —Alan Watts

Imagine the freedom of NOT being attached to those socially inherited constructs!?

THE PAYOFF: BE A SPACE FOR GOOD THINGS TO HAPPEN

Here is the punchline to bring to your everyday life: **Space is more important than the container.** Containers can give you a false sense of wholeness, while wholeness is open to a different future. Wholeness includes the missing parts—what's evolving and what's beyond what you have imagined so far in your life.

Time to take the training wheels off!

Don't let the container limit you!

> "'Wu wei', directly translated, means not overdoing, over-extending, pushing the river, or forcing something to happen. It means we create the environment for something good to come out of it."
>
> —Solala Towler

Solala Towler has taught and practiced Taoist meditation and qigong for over twenty-five years. He is the author of *Tales from the Tao* and *Tao Paths to Love,* among other books, and editor of *The Empty Vessel*, a widely respected journal of Taoist philosophy and practice. Solala was my guest on a *Tao of Pizza* podcast.

He shared with me that "we are not forcing our opinion on other people or forcing ourselves to meditate eight hours a day, or we'll never become enlightened!" You bring your passion and practice to every area of your life, with the understanding that life will have its cycles of ups and downs (yin and yang are always shifting), and you learn to flow with that.

Creating space for good things to happen requires breaking free from limiting containers. It's about embracing wholeness and openness to new possibilities, even if it means leaving behind familiar constructs. Hell, that's a good thing! By shedding outdated beliefs, you make room for new understanding, connection, and experiences.

HERE'S THE (INTER)CONNECTION

Have you ever thought you had something figured out, then you got new information, or a thought that blew your certainty out the window—like finding out there's no Santa Claus? **Breaking the container happens because you don't need that information anymore. You have reached a new level of understanding.**

Once you think you've figured it all out and have this beautiful model, the end is to blow it up because you "got" it. You can move on… to the next elegant step or the next exciting thing. This is why you want to create space instead of filling up a container—it's open and limitless!

In the embrace of wholeness, you discover the true nature of your being, which is at once finite and eternal. In this realization, **you find the courage to transcend the limitations of your constructs and see the boundless horizons of consciousness.** In the expansiveness of your being, you see the freedom to explore the infinite possibilities of existence.

WRAPPIN' IT UP

It's a fact about human nature that we overestimate what can be accomplished in a year, but completely and overwhelmingly *underestimate* what we can accomplish in a decade or two or five. You know how they say, "How time flies"? So, do you want to stay stuck in your safe container, waiting around for life to give its gifts to you and making no difference for yourself or anyone else?

What impossibility that serves humanity will you bring to life in the next ten, twenty, or fifty-plus years you have left? Start that company, publish that book, create that movement that makes a difference in a way that inspires.

> *It's time to dash*
> *for the cash*
> *you said was your dash*
> *and spend your stash*
> *before you become ash...*

GOING DEEPER

Mind-Body Practice for Releasing Powerful Paradigms of the Past (5-7 Minutes)

Ah, the sealed container of the past! Sometimes, it sits quietly, yet its cracks grow, threatening to burst open at any moment. Unresolved past issues are like a bubbling and boiling pressure cooker inside—until the burden becomes too much to hold.

Breaking this container is necessary. Confront what's inside, carefully examine what serves you, and release what doesn't. If needed, seek guidance to help you unpack unnecessary cargo with clarity.

The past can define you and confine you, or it can be a solid foundation for growth. Shatter any and all limits, let go, and step forward in faith—free and unburdened.

Blend mindfulness, breathwork, and movement to generate a breakthrough on whatever holds you back. Release its grip and move forward with strength, clarity, and purpose.

1. Centering Breathwork (2 minutes)

- Sit comfortably or stand with your feet firmly planted on the ground, shoulder width apart.
- Close your eyes and take a slow, deep breath in through the nose, filling your lungs completely.
- Hold for a count of three, then exhale slowly through the mouth.
- As you inhale, silently say, *"I acknowledge the past."*
- As you exhale, say, *"I release what no longer serves me."*
- Repeat for at least five full breaths, allowing your body to relax.

2. Gentle Movement & Release (2 minutes)

- Stand up (if seated) and gently shake out your hands, arms, and legs—imagine shaking off the weight of unresolved issues.
- Slowly roll your shoulders back, releasing tension.
- Stretch your arms wide, opening your chest as if embracing the present.
- Take a deep breath in, bringing your hands to your heart. Exhale and visualize letting go of the past.

3. Visualization for Closure (3 minutes)

- Close your eyes and picture a door in front of you. Behind it lies unresolved past issues.
- Imagine opening the door and seeing those experiences as a book.
- Acknowledge the lessons, then visualize closing the book and placing it on a shelf.
- As you step away, feel a sense of lightness and empowerment.
- Take a final deep breath and say, *"I am free to move forward in faith."*
- Open your eyes and bring gentle movement to your body.

CLOSING REFLECTION

Place both hands over your heart. Take one last deep breath, knowing that the past does not define you—it strengthens you. Step into the present with faith, clarity, and confidence.

Bonus feature: Add a guided mantra or affirmation to reinforce this practice.

NOTES

INNERCHAPTER
THE PRACTICE OF FREEDOM

1969 is a year identified with the transformation of culture, science, and spirituality. We put a man on the moon with intensive science, and more impressively, we brought them back. The sexual revolution, civil rights movements, and drug culture marked a decade painted brightly with color to usher in the freewheelin' '70s that would radically transform America's cultural landscape. Eventually, most of the world was transformed to a new meaning of freedom, marked by the fall of the Berlin Wall in the late 80s.

1969 also ushered in a tremendous amount of spiritual freedom. Eastern practices like meditation, which were marginal in the '50s and '60s with the Beat Generation, started to become mainstream in the '60s. In 1969, the first edition of *Transpersonal Psychology* was published.

The gap between spirituality and science began to diminish with the growing popularity of the publication. In 2000, when I started graduate school, there were only a handful of studies on meditation, and the only famous one was done in—you guessed it—1969. A Harvard doc, Herbert Benson, did a study proving the efficacy of Transcendental Meditation.

Today, there are thousands of studies on meditation every year, reliably creating evidence for the benefits of a consistent practice. Mindfulness, prayer, fasting, gratitude, forgiveness and many other spiritual practices have been verified by science to be effective in creating better health and balanced peace of mind.

Most notable for me is that the theories of Sigmund Freud (who is unanimously considered the "Father of Modern Psychology") have proven to be some of the least reliable psychological theories when held up to scientific inquiry. Humanistic and Transpersonal psychology have come to the party and said, **Let's find out what's useful in all of it, and integrate timeless wisdom with cutting-edge science into lived experience in a practical way.**

The perspectives of holism and unity are central to the worldview of transpersonal psychology because… everything is energy, and we are all connected by energy. Again, calling in Einstein's quote: "Our task must be to free ourselves from this prison by widening our circle of compassion to embrace all living creatures and the whole of nature in its beauty." **Getting to the ultimate source of our energy, vitality and wholeness starts with freedom from the prison that makes us feel separate.**

The Practice of Freedom I have developed is based on the following holistic, mystical, and statistical principles:

- Mindful walking, sitting, strength training, washing dishes, work—all of life as a practice of awakening to the fundamental unity, principles, and patterns of the universe.

- Not a cozy place for the intellect to hang out. The straightforward present-moment awareness and non-judgment, by its nature, devalues the discursive intellect of words and abstract theories. It creates a space for imagination, curiosity, and compassionate action.
- Not dependent upon sitting on a pillow to practice. Value the simple, concrete living facts of everyday direct personal experience. Go about your day mindful of intention, self-reliance, self-discipline, personal effort, and interdependency.
- The inner journey is a prelude to going outward.
- Based on this soul (and sole) purpose: *BEing joy and compassion to mingle in the world "with helping hands."*

CHAPTER NINE

COMMUNITY LENS— CONTRIBUTION

[Re]Connecting to community with strength, unity, and resilience

> "Life is short. Eternity is real, and relationships matter most."
>
> —Pastor Dave Patterson

In the history of human existence, the concept of community has woven its threads through the ages. It has been a fundamental element of social life for thousands of years. In fact, 3000 years ago, we wouldn't even be talking about "community" because it was inherent and assumed—that's all there was. THAT's how intrinsic society was in the strength of connection and communal bonds.

How times have changed!

We confront the paradoxical reality that, unlike our ancestors of 3000 years past, we find ourselves distanced from the very concept we once took for granted. It seems we've **regressed instead of advanced as civilized social beings when "community" isn't as natural to us as living and breathing.**

Walking on a street almost anywhere in the world, you'll observe most people walking alone or with others with their faces buried in their "smart" phones instead of looking at each other. It's natural for people to avoid—even be afraid of—interacting with others in public places. ChatGPT (yes, I consulted an inanimate bunch of bytes instead of asking somebody) identified over thirty articles published by *Psychology Today* in one year (2023), specifically dedicated to the topic of the *negative psychological impacts of loneliness in our society!*

What does this mean for us today that, in our contemporary landscape, it feels unnatural or even impossible to foster genuine connections? How can we rediscover and rekindle the collaborative spirit that once bound us together in the tapestry of shared human experience?

The concept of community as inherent and intrinsic now stands as a beacon calling us back to a collective consciousness that has been lost in the currents of modernity.

BACK TO BASICS: WE BE TREES!

I turn to nature again to remind us of who we are. As you recall, scientists now know that trees can communicate with each other using the "Woodwide Web" to share resources, help the struggling young saplings grow, and send out distress signals about drought or disease. Each tree is growing while helping others grow so the whole community can thrive. Trees do this because that's who they are. They don't forget, they don't withhold, and they're not afraid.

Somewhere along the line, we humans have developed an image of being separate, thinking that being independent is a good thing. But that's not true—a single human couldn't exist on their own! While we know that each one of us is whole—an intact unit or entity that is complete in itself—we ALSO know we are part of a community and of every other living thing.

With all the tools we humans have, we should be able to nail this! Just look at the ones we've explored in this book:

- We have amazing spiritual gifts we can tap into to BE our best selves.
- We know the power of our energy, feelings, thoughts, and actions when we use them with intention and integrity.
- We have the awareness that we are part of a bigger whole, a collective, a community. And now we know that community is not a foregone conclusion in our society today.

It's imperative to be intentional about how we function with each other and contribute to community. **How do we ensure that we** *are making positive contributions, building great relationships, and having fun in the communities we belong to?*

Connecting with people who want to grow, learn, and create is the biggest passion I have in life. Building relationships that thrive is at the heart of everything I am—and everything this book has been about.

Another way of saying it is: "I AM the commitment to building quality, trust-based relationships." We usually don't talk that way (even the grammar tool on Word doesn't like it!). **High-quality relationships contribute so much to creating an outstanding life.**

So, let's start with our personal relationships, and I'll lead with this story:

> **My dad invested the last decade of his life** serving the community of Alcoholics Anonymous (AA), the global fellowship dedicated to recovery from substance use disorders, behavioral addictions, and other co-occurring mental health conditions. When Dad was in his mid-sixties, his doctor raised health concerns about his drinking and recommended that he quit. I never thought of my dad as a heavy drinker. He did the smart thing and found a different doctor :-).
>
> This doctor told him he couldn't continue this way anymore. He was promised only six months to live. In my dad's words, the second doctor was a

bigger asshole than the first—but he started to get that his health was being threatened. I think about how Dad could've said, *Screw you,* and continued on as usual, and I respect that he chose to take the doc's advice and enroll in an HMO group program about alcohol and substance abuse.

Through those workshops, he began meeting people in AA and started his healing path to sobriety and service to the group. Dad was sixty-eight when he got sober and lived ten more healthy, quality years.

Dad and I had been estranged for nearly a decade. As I've mentioned, he stopped paying child support the day I turned eighteen, even though he had promised to pay for my college tuition. Some interesting things were said between him and my mother, so I cut ties and made it my mission to do it on my own.

One gift of my spiritual journey happened when I realized I didn't want my kids to be denied the opportunity to have a relationship with their grandparents, as I had. So, I worked through my resentment toward my dad and finally approached him to patch things up. It worked out with him and my stepmother, and things were good between us.

You're likely familiar with AA's 12-Step Program and its recovery practices. One of the steps involves reconciling relationships. As part of the AA steps, I decided to confront my dad about withdrawing his support, believing he might be in a good place to have the conversation.

I asked him why he broke his word. He first acknowledged that he did make that promise, which I appreciated. He told me his health affected his income at that time. He chose to change careers because of the toll that stress was taking on his body—something I'd never known before.

The final thing he said was the clincher, "And I thought you had it all figured out. You had everything under control." This was news to me! I had believed all along that he didn't care about me or what I had accomplished. Tears started streaming down my cheeks. My heart opened wide, and I felt nothing but compassion for my dad.

All I ever wanted to prove in my life was the fact that "I had it all figured out." My dad's words not only took responsibility for the breach; they affirmed me. I felt deeply understood.

Because I'd spent so many years harboring resentment and pain, I was blinded to the inherent connection that is essential for two family members to have—trees connected through the same roots. In the world of estranged relationships, I know I'm one of the lucky ones, thanks to my spiritual practices and my dad's involvement with the AA community, which led us to this transformational moment.

Being intentional in integrity and love—along with understanding how we humans are as connected as the trees in a forest—we begin to weave those threads that will build into meaningful personal and professional relationships.

On the personal level, community is the basic principle of the Golden Rule. The Hiddle-Haddle version: ***Try to love your neighbors like you love yourself, including the people who piss you off—most importantly, the ones who piss you off!!***

It's really hard to do, and that's the whole point.

HARNESSING THE POWER OF COMMUNITY GATHERING

Drawing inspiration from my spiritual teachers and guides over the years and blending my Christian beliefs with Taoist philosophy, I believe in the transformative potential of community.

> "The next Buddha will manifest not in one person but in a collective, a sangha."
>
> —Thích Nhất Hạnh

Thích Nhất Hạnh is known as the main inspiration for engaged Buddhism, bridging Eastern and Western thought and practice. By this statement, he meant to emphasize the ***importance of community in achieving enlightenment and fostering spiritual growth.*** Instead of focusing on the individual, he highlighted the collective power of a harmonious and supportive group that supports each other's spiritual journey and embodies principles of mindfulness, compassion, and interconnectedness.

This idea of sangha underscores the belief that enlightenment is not just a solo sport; it is a shared experience nurtured through communal effort and mutual support.

So, I say, *why just leave it to the spiritual practitioners?*

We ALL can bring our own versions of sangha into our everyday lives, at home and at work!

Social connection is one of the most powerful aspects of a healthy lifestyle for so many reasons:

- *Mutual encouragement* protects us and motivates us to get up when we fall.
- *Sharing and witnessing testimony* generates an unrivaled healing process. We identify blind spots and sharpen our gifts.
- *Spiritual gifts are best developed in a community.* "For where two or more are gathered in my name..." (Matthew 18:20) is one of my favorite Bible verses. God will show up and release the gifts of spirit into your life.
- *Access to wise counsel* equips us to share our ministry and develop greater spiritual victories through collaboration and partnership.
- *Collective strength and encouragement* offer the freedom to become an instrument of peace with our finances, so we control our money instead of it controlling us.
- *Community reveals the light of the world.*

NETWORKING IS NOT WORKING

It's not that networking DOESN'T work; instead, it is NOT work, but simply the unlimited access to the powerful concepts of *distributed cognition* and *collective intelligence*.

Coming out of cognitive science and psychology, "distributed cognition" is the idea that cognitive processes aren't confined to one individual's mind but are distributed across people, their environment and their technologies—another not-so-crazy concept about connectivity and not too far off from the network of trees that "know" how to support and nourish each other to survive and grow.

"Collective intelligence" is the shared knowledge, insights, and problem-solving ability that happens when a group works together, in which more is accomplished as a group than could be achieved by a single individual. Here's more on that, as well as a shoutout to Michele Carroll, one of my guests on The Tao of Pizza Podcast and an exemplary example of this concept:

> **International Society of Service Innovation Professionals** (ISSIP) is a diverse global community of thousands that together advance service innovation to benefit people, businesses, and society as a whole. ISSIP provides "a platform for knowledge exchange, dissemination and programs... that help people do better for our interconnected world." Their mission and work embody "collective intelligence."

Michele Carroll, founder and president of Carrollco Marketing Services and Executive Director of ISSIP, has been at the forefront of business innovation for decades. Her marketing teams have secured millions in funding, helped companies gain market traction and grow the US market.

According to Michele, service innovation should remain people-centered. While tech is beneficial to the marketplace, human connection—often supported by technology for efficiency—is what drives business and society.

Distributed cognition... collective intelligence... What better descriptors could there be for networking?

Throughout history, cultures have recognized and harnessed the power of collective energy, believing it to influence both the material and spiritual realms. For example, the Chinese concept of and practices around an energy force (qi) that flows through all living things.

What all this means to me is that **when you bring multiple minds together, you create this higher mind. It belongs to everyone, and everyone has access and contributes to it. The result is an increased ability to accomplish goals and innovate.** And it benefits everyone, individually and as a whole.

Through our Spiritual Lens, we experience and practice how we see the parts, the whole, and the possibility of seeing with energy, so that we have a boundless appreciation of what community can be.

Through our Emotional Lens, we are in touch with our emotions and thought patterns so that we can show up for our community from a clear, healthy, mindful place, giving and receiving each other's wisdom.

Through our Mental Lens, we are accountable to others, and they're accountable to us. We keep our commitments to the best of our ability. There doesn't have to be 100% perfection here: *Hey, I did commit to that. It didn't happen. How's that gonna affect the group? And how do I get current right now?* We get to choose our language—how we talk to ourselves and other people. Our words roll into action.

> **I was working with my team on applying** the concept of their Mental Lens. One of the exercises I led was to help them clarify what they wanted to commit to doing better and to keep agreements with themselves on doing those things. Everybody wrote down a set of affirmations, and we shared them in the group.
>
> Hank started reading his out loud, and every one of them began with the phrase, "I have to…" I gently interrupted him to suggest a little tweak: "What if you started your affirmation with, 'I CHOOSE to…' instead of 'I HAVE to…'?"
>
> He began to read them again, paused, then his eyes lit up like firecrackers as he realized what a difference the simple change of a word made! Knowing you have the freedom to choose, not a

forced obligation, opens up opportunity and fun. That's speaking your world into existence!

Through our Action Lens, we create something that's a resource to the community and is self-generating. One person doesn't have to do it all—we have each other's backs. Everyone can take ownership of the successes. When everyone keeps their agreements and does their part, it creates synergy, and it feels great!

Through the Economic Lens, we see business as a living system, we serve selflessly, and innovate continuously within the group. Money is the energy that connects us all, and we circulate it for the benefit of the group (our family, business, volunteer groups, local community, and throughout the planet).

Through the Effort Lens, we practice *flex and flow* and create a space for good things to happen. We don't listen to our egos telling us to take over every situation, and we exercise patience in listening to and working with each other.

> **In our business, some of our clients want** to use their own resources or teams, such as an engineering department that knows their business better than we ever could. I hear about companies that don't want to work that way, but we believe that the end result is better when talented heads are put together. We feel confident that we can work on the whole picture and let them facilitate the parts they specialize in. I don't feel threatened; instead, I'm excited about the better outcomes that can happen in a partnership. And I practice being an Agent of Chill.

Through the Attunement Lens, we learn through working with other people. With everyone's access to the higher mind, we get to tap into others' knowledge, talents, expertise, and passions. We use this new knowledge to increase our own abilities and fine-tune our Whole Person Paradigm practice.

So, networking becomes something different from our connotations of finding the most lucrative events, working the room, automating LinkedIn responses, and looking for immediate ROI from every encounter—you know, hard work and not fun!

We want to open ourselves to opportunities for synergy wherever they might arise and put relationships first—authentic relationships. We want to get together with multiple minds and hearts to do and BE something greater than ourselves.

> "You ARE your network."
>
> —Michael (Mick) Mankowski

Mick Mankowski was my dad's best friend, and I hosted him on my *Tao of Pizza* podcast. This guy is my hero. He made all these multimillion-dollar deals and companies, went broke twice, and still rose from the ashes to be successful again. He told me that you are your network; your contacts are your Rolodex (metaphorically speaking these days)—that's who you are. To me, this means we aren't the self-reliant egos we think we are. We need each other. As we have been talking about throughout this book, relationships are an essential part of who we are, in business and personal life.

THE PAYOFF: PARADOX OF STRUCTURE GENERATING FREEDOM

In the spirit of expanding the edges of consciousness, let's look at the lowly meeting. Why do we love to hate meetings? Choose your favorite reasons... Bottom line, I think the main reason is that a lot of meetings are a waste of time—they are constricting, we hear the same thing from the same people over and over, there's no chance for creative thinking or humor and you feel like you're in a cage and want to break out.

In the last chapter, we talked about breaking free from conventional models. I can't think of anything more conventional than meetings. What if we were to burst the boundaries of the meetings we've known and been bored with for years? **What if a meeting were an intentionally designed construct that encourages freedom to connect, communicate, and distribute cognition?**

Here's the thing: We do need meetings. There are times when people have to get together to design something, share information, agree on processes and goals, learn stuff, etc. I recognize the paradox of proposing a structure for meetings that generates freedom, but stay with me here...

1. The first five minutes of each gathering serve as a mindful transition into the space. The intention is to invite and allow members to immerse themselves in the present moment. The facilitator/leader offers an exercise or ritual that incorporates various practices like poetry, visualizations, and silent or guided meditation. These structured practices evolve over weeks to align with the group's project or objective and with their growth as a community of sorts.

2. The core of the meeting has these elements (Note: the leader is facilitating, NOT dictating or lecturing to the members):

- Conscious accountability in pursuit of clarity within the group
- Clear and defined expectations are outlined to encourage full participation and open exchange without judgment
- Encouragement to openly contribute and expand their ways of being
- Feedback, which means exchanging with each other, is rooted in grounded observations rather than advice, becoming a tool not just for the next action steps but also for personal and group growth

3. The concluding three minutes involve a round-robin recap, creating a space for shared insights and reflections.

4. The group concludes with an emphasis on using failure as motivation to try again (fostering resilience) and a commitment to improvement in pursuing excellence—concepts rooted in the most important practice: *love*.

My initial resistance to creating a "structure" dissolved once I started seeing the role of a meeting as promoting self-awareness, aligning values and intention, and increasing engaged participation—that gets things done!

HERE'S THE (INTER)CONNECTION

> "History has shown that any man who would significantly change the world must have showmanship, a general willingness to shed other people's blood, and a plausible new religion to introduce during the brief period of repentance that always follows bloodshed."
>
> —*Prof. Kurt Vaughn*

By far, my most engaging and instructive teacher was Professor Kurt Vaughn, an adjunct faculty member in the Sacramento State Philosophy department. It was rumored that he was a secret agent. He altered my opinion regarding social change for good.

Prof. Vaughn loved to reference Kurt Vonnegut's satirical essay, "Tyranny with a Difference," from his 1963 book, *Cat's Cradle*. Vonnegut imagines a dystopian future where a computer named EPICAC XIV governs society with seemingly flawless logic. However, the system devolves into a cold and oppressive regime. **The story warns of "perfect" systems that promise to fix social problems but ultimately perpetuate tyranny in new forms.**

Inspired by that essay, I created a Hiddle-Haddle version about a fictional place called Danger Island:

The leaders of Danger Island dreamed of making it a utopia, so they overhauled the economy and laws. Rear Admiral Chris Johnson designed a new "religion": Pertinacious Practice of Peace and Prosperity.

He wanted all things to fit together so people could be happy in every sense. The world they had inherited seemed angry and tense. And he made their sad world a paradise.

However, Johnson's superiors on the island believed that good societies could be built only by pitting good against evil and keeping the tension high between the two at all times. To that end, Johnson's peace-evoking religion was eventually outlawed. Statutes were instituted. One of them was that anyone caught sharing the Practice of Peace would be prosecuted to the full extent of the law. They outlawed the practice of peace.

Welcome to tyranny with a difference! If you created a religion or system in which everything worked and everybody agreed and was on the same side, things would be great—Utopian—for a while. But humans being humans and power being power, as the religion grew and expanded, somewhere along the line, there would be conflict. It soon becomes tyranny bait.

See any similarities today? If you dig a little into almost any structure—religion, government, media, business, sports, the arts—you will see power concentration, greed, divided factions, good decisions gone wrong, and bad decisions even worse.

In other words, *ego reflects the opposite of community.*

Remember Airbnb in its beginnings? In 2007, some guys who were struggling to pay rent decided to convert their San Francisco, CA, loft into a lodging space for attendees of a design conference who couldn't find hotel rooms. They provided air mattresses and breakfast, hence the name "Air Bed & Breakfast." It was so successful and rewarding for everybody involved that they saw the potential of connecting people who needed reasonable lodging with people who had their couches, spare rooms, or homes to offer. It was a beautiful kind of couch-surfing grassroots thing, where people could interchange and act with each other in ways that were never before possible. It was also a great example of the concept of "shared economy."

Over time, Airbnb grew into a global phenomenon, revolutionizing the hospitality industry. And along the way, things changed out of a confluence of issues (mostly based on ego-driven greed). According to reporting by Vox, a flood of hosts began entering the market from a viral, hyped-up dream of striking it rich. In a period of low-interest mortgage rates, amateur investors saturated the market by buying up properties to turn into short-term rentals. You would have thought that excess supply would have brought prices down, but hosts' expenses then climbed in a period of inflation, and so did their fees, especially as property managers began to enter the market, hiking up rental prices. Extreme demands and rules began to increase, and quality control went out the window because of dishonest hosts and the company's inability to stay ahead of it all.

The company began to get "corporatized." Their service fees steadily increased to 14% on top of the nightly rate, in addition to 3% from the hosts—while raking in almost $2 billion in profits in 2022. "Airbnb began as a more flexible, more social experience than hotels, but that sense of peer-to-peer exchange has all but disappeared," says Whizty Kim, writing for Vox.

As you're out there building synergies, relationships and communities, bear in mind that things can get screwed up when they engender conflict, get corporatized, leaders get power-hungry and greedy, and structures outlive their usefulness and start to go south. We want to trust government and companies and world organizations and leaders, and we can choose to—they're all essential parts of community. Just be aware that none are perfect, and discernment is helpful. AND you have the power and choice to do it differently.

The antidote? **Use all your Lenses and extraordinary human gifts to discern and make mindful choices.**

Another tip: **I believe a thriving, healthy community is best when it acts locally and allows its influence to go global.** Start where you are, in your own place and own situation, to BE the difference that makes a difference. Here's an example that's especially close to my heart ...

Have you seen the movie *American Graffiti*? It's a nostalgic look at the 1960s, directed by George Lucas (his first critical and commercial success), in which a group of teenagers "spend one final night after their 1962 high school graduation cruising the strip with their buddies before they pursue their varying goals."

The movie was set in Modesto, California, my hometown and George Lucas' birthplace. Chris Murphy (remember him, the fearless karaoke singer?) lives in Modesto; in fact, he is Mr. Modesto! Chris is a true Renaissance Man, CEO and president of a third-generation business, Sierra Pacific Warehouse Group, publisher of the *ModestoView*, musician, cruise enthusiast, and supporter and active community builder. The guy never stops!

Along with a group of enthusiasts, Chris co-founded the Graffiti USA Museum, which celebrates American Graffiti culture (classic streetscape of cars, art, music, history, and pop culture) and the Graffiti USA Classic Car Museum. These museums attract people from all over the world.

After the success of "American Graffiti," people from across the country came to Modesto to participate in cruising events. If you don't know what cruising is, it's where people—car enthusiasts, bored teenagers, low-rider car clubbers, et al—drive slowly up and down downtown streets to show off their cars and socialize.

In 1990, Modesto enacted a ban to outlaw cruising. City officials saw it as a contributor to traffic congestion, noise, and crime (gang fights and shootings). It was a community gathering gone wrong—but so was the short-sighted solution.

In the early 2020s, Chris was part of a grassroots effort to revive this aspect of Modesto's history, lobbying the city to argue that cruising was a vital part of Modesto's identity and a potential economic boon. I once spotted a giant sign on the side of the street with my buddy's face on it that said *NO CRUISE BAN*. The beauty was that different factions and cultures came together for this effort: local car clubs, nostalgic residents, business owners, and supporters of Modesto's cultural heritage—even police officers, including the police chief. People realized the ban was unenforceable, and when it was enforced, it targeted the low-rider guys, some of whom did jail terms. Even one of the city council members said that the cruising ban was rooted in racism and an outdated perception of gang culture.

On July 17, 2023, members of seventeen car clubs and other interested citizens filled the city council chambers to voice their support. The low-riders club itself stated its commitment to keep out the "wrong element" in order to maintain safety in the streets! During public comment, Chris Murphy said, "When we bring our cultures together, our community shines. This is good for our town."

The city council voted to lift the cruising ban, and community events have been held since to celebrate Modesto's culture and storied automotive history, including cruising.

For Chris, it's fundamentally about "Serving Civic Pride Daily" and making sure his company, family, and employees are engaged and connected "to make our company and community better for us and the next generation." Recently, I attended one of these events because Chris was going to be honored for his community service. The Chief of Police of Modesto presented him with the award. Funny sidebar: He receives his award, and his band joins him to play for the rest of the event!

THIS is what community connection and service can look like.

WRAPPIN' IT UP: A POSITIVE VISION FOR HUMANKIND

This hopeful vision comes with a balanced and resilient practice for living in these times. In this book, we've acquired some fundamentals of a path along which we develop and integrate our many-sided natures. It points us toward realizing our greater capacities and encourages us to develop our gifts in response to the opportunities around us.

Underpinned by love, our practice can guide us as we advance into a more extraordinary life. Drawing from the wisdom traditions of the past and harnessing knowledge gained from scientific discoveries, we generate the possibility of a new worldview.

The context of our lives gets expanded to one of exploration and adventure (with humor and fun!). Humankind participates in a universal, transformative expansion, and we each play our unique role in that progression. We choose to experience the joy of being wholly ourselves and wholly connected to the cosmic system of which we are an integral part.

Who we are and what we do matters—all part of the path to deep peace, unshakable clarity, and true prosperity.

The door is open. I invite you to join me on this ultimate adventure!

GOING DEEPER

Tapping into Collective Intelligence through Community
(5–7 minutes to enhance your perspective and start developing your ecosystem)

Step 1: Set an intention (1 minute)

Close your eyes, take a deep breath, and ask yourself:

What do I want to create, solve, or accomplish right now?
Hold that vision clearly in your mind. Feel with all six senses, the excitement of it—not as something you must do alone, but something that becomes possible *with others*.

Step 2: Identify your community needs (2 minutes)

On paper or in your notes app, or in this book, answer these prompts:

- Who already inspires or supports me?
- What knowledge, skills, or resources would help move my vision forward?
- What type of energy or mindset do I want around me?

This list of abilities and resources becomes your *ecosystem-building blueprint.*

Step 3: Take one connection action (2 minutes)

Choose a straightforward action to plug into collective intelligence today:

- Join an online forum, industry, or local group related to your goal
- Message someone you admire and ask a thoughtful question
- Express your community intention with a trusted friend or colleague
- Offer a skill or insight to someone in your network

Step 4: Close with a visualization (2 minutes)

Close your eyes again. Picture yourself at the center of a living web, where each thread represents a connection—support, inspiration, knowledge. See the web lighting up as you reach out, share, and receive. Feel the power of *not doing it alone.*

Affirm to yourself:

I am part of something bigger. I give, receive, and grow with others. Together, anything is possible.

Let this be your reminder: Community isn't something you "find"—it's something you *create and co-create.*

NOTES

INNERCHAPTER
THE NATURAL EVOLUTION OF SOCIAL, ECONOMIC, AND STRUCTURAL NETWORKS
(a history)

Our civilizations change over time. But what about our psychologies? According to one theory of human development, despite our unique natures, we are malleable enough to become more complex people within more complex societies.

Oh yeah, we're about to machete through some serious weeds...

Societies resemble self-organizing network processes, or "spontaneous orders"—complex, adaptive, nonlinear systems that evolve, transform, and become more complex, all without anyone purposefully organizing them.

Interestingly, as it happens in societies, so it goes in our individual development. Because human brains are also complex networks, we develop psychologically as children do, through identifiable stages that form increasingly complex psychological levels. The growth may continue throughout a lifetime. The idea is that when a society contains a critical number of people at a given stage, it transforms, creating the social conditions for another psychological developmental stage.

The SD model provides a valuable framework for understanding the relationship between social and individual development.

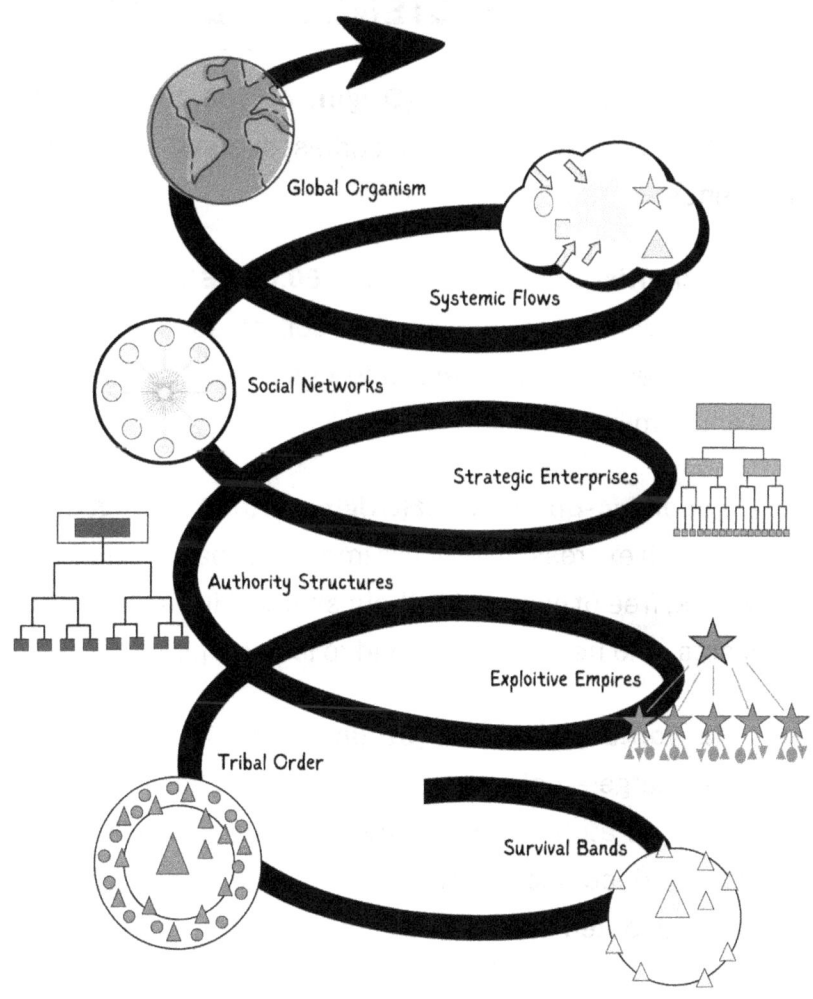

Let's take a cursory walk through the Tier One stages to examine social and individual evolution through the SD lens. A different color represents each stage. We'll zip through the social evolution representation to give you some context, then go deeper into what is actually the whole theme of this book—*a holistic look at yourself in Whole Person terms.*

TIER ONE: SUBSISTENCE AND ORDER

Beige – *Archaic-instinctive* **(Origin: c. 100,000 BC):** Self-centered, survivalist stage as our earliest expression of self and subsistence.

Purple – *Animistic-tribal* **(Origin: c. 50,000 BC):** Collectivist, tribal stage where the individual becomes subsumed in the group, the ways of the elders, and customs. Life centers on friend and family bonds.

Red – *Egocentric-dominionist* **(Origin: c. 7,000 BC):** Egocentric stage in which expression of self is impulsive, based on what the self desires, free of guilt and without shame. Humans celebrate heroic acts, and heroic figures tend to lead empires.

Blue – *Authoritarian-mythic* **(Origin: c. 3,000 BC):** Out of empire arises larger-scale communitarian life, essentially held together by an authoritarian superstructure characterized by personal sacrifice and obedience, often guarded by brutal authorities and rooted in myth.

Orange – *Multiplistic-scientific/strategic* **(Origin: c. 1,000 AD):** A more socially-minded but decidedly individualistic psychology emerges in this stage, best exemplified by the Industrial Revolution, the Renaissance, the Age of Reason, and modern capitalism.

Green – *Relativistic-egalitarian* (Origin: 1850 on, surging early 20th century): Self-interest shifts to gain acceptance, group inclusion, and social harmony. Socialism, existentialism, and postmodernism are typical of this stage, often exemplified by the 1960s. What emerges is a kind of balancing between atomistic individualism and authoritarian collectivism.

TIER TWO: BEING AND ORDER

Now, we get into the meat of the thing. **Tier Two represents social-psychological expression in which humanity is no longer in a reactive survival mode**—from *how do I live and organize* toward *who am I and how do I relate?* Each successive stage is a reaction to the pathologies of the previous stage, ostensibly to grow into "new and improved" versions, attempting to integrate ALL stages.

Because the brain is a constantly active and changing, self-organizing network, we should expect to see such a transformation process happen over time. And because society is a network of communicating brains, we can also expect to see social transformation as an emergent phenomenon, reflecting these psychological stages. Elegant interconnectivity!

Let's compare the Tier One paradigm to a group of passengers on a train. Orange is looking out one side of the train and saying,

Hey! We need to be more self-reliant and reward individuals who excel in generating value for their communities. Green is looking out the other side and saying, *Whoa! We need to preserve our ecological resources and realize their true value, and we need to ensure a certain level of rights for all individuals.*

In Tier One, we're in constant battles over who is right about what's happening on either side of the train. It's not until Tier Two that a significant number of people look at each other and say, **Holy shit! We need to get out in front of this thing and start laying a new track!!**

Holistic systems thinkers accept that our tribal origins, authority structures, and strategic enterprises are part of our present reality, not to reject or re-invent but to build upon. Enter Tier-Two Yellow and Turquoise, which represent the crux of the principles in this book:

Yellow – *Systemic-integrative* (Origin: 1950s): Self-expression is not so much about what the self desires as it is about avoiding harm to others so that all life benefits. Something interesting happens here: A more individualistic self understands its place within a complex, dynamic, and evolutionary world. **People should be understood as responsible and free, but freedom must be reconciled and integrated within wider systems of self.**

Someone like Bucky Fuller comes along and says, *Look, it's not a train, it's a fucken spaceship, and none of us are passengers. We're all an integral part of the crew.*

Turquoise – *Holistic (Origin: 1970s)*: The final stage we can identify is an integrative one, which combines an organism's necessary self-interest with the interests of the communities and subsystems in which it participates. The theory is still forming, but Turquoise tends to understand the world as fully integrated, **with the individual contributing to the social as the social contributes to the individual in a seamless whole.**

ON THE WHOLE PERSON LEVEL...

Here's where it gets really interesting, which is why the SD model warrants attention: *We humans may reflect characteristics of any or many of these stages!* For example, I'm super Orange in business, steeped in technology and innovation. Yet, my team and I can get into survival mode, working together as a tribe (Purple) with our own traditions and culture. As a father, I may be Blue—an authority figure—or Red (a tyrant sometimes, at least according to my kids...).

This next section covers the stages (colors) from the personal (Whole Person) point of view. As you read this next section, think about how the aspects of each color might relate to your worldview and personal life.

Beige: Survival Bands. A person stranded in a harsh environment, like a shipwreck survivor who is focused entirely on securing food and safety. People experiencing homelessness or extreme poverty may also operate primarily from this survival-based level.

Purple: Tribal Order. Someone who believes in luck, superstitions, or rituals to protect their family and honor their ancestors. A person who is deeply connected to their cultural heritage and family traditions may express these values in a close-knit community setting. Many may be overly committed to the limited constructs that govern their lives.

Red: Exploitative Empires. A rebellious teenager who seeks to prove their independence through risky behaviors, or a street gang member asserting dominance and respect through aggression. An entrepreneur or leader with a "my way or the highway" approach, often driven by ego and the pursuit of personal glory.

Blue: Authority Structure. A devout religious follower who strictly adheres to religious texts, or a law-abiding citizen who believes strongly in societal rules and the importance of hierarchy. A soldier who respects the chain of command and believes in the honor of serving their country.

Orange: Strategic Enterprises. An entrepreneur focused on building a successful business, using strategic thinking and innovation to get ahead. A scientist dedicated to breakthroughs and research, motivated by personal recognition and advancement. Someone who invests in self-improvement and goal setting.

Green: Social Networks. An environmental activist who advocates for sustainable practices or a social worker devoted to helping underprivileged communities. Someone passionate about social causes, such as LGBTQ+ rights, feminism, or racial equality, who prioritizes relationships and emotional well-being over individual self-interest.

Yellow: Systemic Flows. A holistic systems thinker seeking to solve complex problems by understanding all interrelated parts, or an innovator working on projects integrating technology and nature. Someone who prioritizes continuous learning and self-actualization, understanding that different perspectives are valuable.

Turquoise: Global Organization. A global thinker who focuses on the interconnectedness of all life and works on initiatives to protect the planet. Visionaries like the Dalai Lama or environmental leaders like Vandana Shiva advocate for global harmony and spiritual and ecological balance. A meditator who experiences a sense of unity with the universe.

I hope you find this Spiral Dynamics concept as fascinating as I do for exploring the natural progression of what has been, where you are, and what you can be in all the different phases of life.

You can also view this framework in terms of community. Take a bird's-eye look at communities you know and where they fall in the dynamic. Explore the perspective (colors) of someone you disagree with, perhaps realizing that it's not a behavior coming out of nowhere, which might allow you to appreciate the value of it and of them.

Arts & Crafts Exercise: *Which combination of colors most accurately represents you right now?* You could design a (pizza?) pie chart representing the colors in percentages, as relates to you, your team, family, business, or community. Fun and insightful possibilities are endless: See how one relates to the other; discover which color you wish you had more of, or less of; find synergies with others so you can learn how the group/family functions together.

NOTES

THE END... AND AN INVITATION TO BEGIN

Are you ready to awaken to your fullest potential?

People experience the need to grow deep in their being, a longing to become more profound, authentic expressions of who they are. The consistent impulse to grow and self-transcend moves both through us and through our world. Our health and the health of our world are deeply intertwined. *The urge that generates our will to develop personally and the universe's natural process are the same.*

Important thoughts to mull and meditate on... but first, let me step back a minute and congratulate you! Welcome to the community. YOU'RE IN—you made it to the END!! I hope you love what you've read so far, and I also hope you're a little pissed off (because both—all—are part of the ebb-and-flow, breaking-constructs and moving-in-and-out-of-comfort zones nature of the path).

Now, let's return to that consistent impulse to self-transcend moving through you. Surrender to that impulse—yours and the world's. Bask in the urge to develop personally toward becoming a more and more authentic expression of YOU.

This has been the purpose and promise of the book, and this is your invitation to begin. In this chapter, I want to leave you with a dynamic set of tools to start on your own Whole Person Paradigm path.

Summing up, the promises and practices of the Whole Person path look like this:

1. When you see things differently, you'll see different things. Through your Lenses and extraordinary human gifts, expand the possibilities, harness your passion and pursuit, and speak your truth.

2. Freedom from the social script. Challenge those things you've taken for granted or have never questioned. Create your own path from a whole-person perspective instead of from well-worn constructs that won't serve you.

3. Balance between art and science. The most cutting-edge practices are spiritual in nature and underpinned by evidence-based and time-tested principles. Embrace them all from an "everything's interconnected" perspective.

4. Walky-walky. Actions speak louder than words. BE your practice. Transform complaints into collaborative solutions. Begin to activate your highest potential for peace and prosperity by taking small, intentional steps in your everyday life.

5. **The Tao of Pizza.** Look at the whole Kosmos with awe and wonder while also finding that same kind of awe and wonder in the tiniest little slices of life that happen every day. THAT's what the Hokey-Pokey is all about!

SPIRITUAL FITNESS: ALIGNING WITH THE UNIVERSE

Vicki Dello Joio is one of my favorite teachers. She is a Qigong Master Teacher and expert on what she has coined "spiritual fitness." She says, "When we work to align ourselves on every level, from physical to emotional to mental to spiritual... we open an enormous well-spring of resources." Both in her work and her book, *The Way of Joy*, Vicki explores many of the themes from ancient Taoist practices and Chinese medicine on cultivating lifeforce energy or qi (chi) through energy work, Qigong, breath work, meditations, Taoist yoga healing, and martial arts. In her Way of Joy system, she has developed what she calls *"the Three Realms of Consciousness"—Heaven, Human and Earth.*

These three realms are primary portals to our connection to the universe and our experience in life. In short, the Heaven Realm contains consciousness and inspiration (where we get our ideas, whether it's intuition, prayer, inspiration, or creativity). The Human Realm contains intention and love (how we bring those visions to life), and the Earth Realm incorporates empowerment and manifestation (our foundation, literally and figuratively, where we feel our place in the universe and draw strength and stability from it).

I invite you to be aware that **you are manifesting heaven here on earth**. Practice with intention and utilize these realms (however you want to name them) as sources of inspiration, manifestation, and power.

I'm a novice practitioner at this, but Vicki is an expert who has brought these amazing ideas to thousands of people to support us in our goals, our purpose, and whatever we want to manifest. It's not an ethic that belongs to any one religion—it's much bigger than that.

This is your invitation to bring heaven to earth. Bam! I just gave you the secret power to everything.

Okay, it's your turn to take it and run...

FROM SELF-SERVING TO SELFLESS SERVICE

First of all, self-service isn't selfish, but many of us worry about this like a dog with a bone. Back in the early chapters, we talked about knowing, expressing, and communicating love in all its forms—and the foundation is self-love. You put on your own oxygen mask before helping your fellow passengers with theirs. You develop your own gifts to serve others (which is the real gift). What is created is a beautiful *expanding cycle of service:* to self and others, which reciprocates to the self, to more and different service to others, and on and on.

For years, I've been beating a well-worn path toward a more extraordinary life. Sometimes, I have felt guilty about taking too much time for myself; sometimes, I've felt like I needed to do it alone without anybody's help. I was mistaken on both counts.

Case in point: writing this book...

The time and effort I've invested in writing and publishing this book in the last many years has impacted my family life—especially my wife. The love I've had for this project is like "the other woman." I've ghosted many conversations because I was game-planning some aspect of this project through mental gymnastics (daydreaming). My wife has been a fantastic source of ideas and support, and I have felt selfish and guilty about being so preoccupied.

However, as the years have passed, I've begun to realize the urge that has motivated me to do this is not all about me. What has literally kept me going to complete the book is thinking about the people who are supporting me and the people I think might get something out of reading it.

Another expression of guilt comes from internalizing the expectations that *I'm supposed to be able to do it all myself.* After years of mulling and stewing over a book idea, putting together chapters, setting down notes, and missing my own ridiculously ambitious completion deadlines, I realized I couldn't do it all myself and was selfish to think I could! The outcome? An amazing collaborative and reciprocal effort that has allowed me to include people I love and respect, collaborate with my kids, meet new people, use these lessons in my team meetings, and maybe someday have a positive effect on people I have never met.

So, what started out as selfish became selfless. Yet, selfishly, I feel like I'm getting a greater reward from the experience—it's a trap! *Am I selfish or selfless??* Well, in the interconnectedness of all beings, we are both things when we touch others with our gifts and superpowers. And the most selfless things happen when they come from self-love.

This is the beautiful, expanding cycle of service. Being connected to and contributing to the greater community fuels the quest to BEing a path toward peace and prosperity.

IN THE SPIRIT OF WALKY-WALKY, TAKE ACTION!!

The gazillion-dollar question is: ***How will you use your dash?***

What is the company you've always wanted to start? The movement you feel passionate about? The relationship you want to start, reconcile, or nurture? The book you're going to write?

You get to choose what you want to be involved in, why, and with whom. Which brings us again to community as stepping stones on the path to whole-personhood.

Family, chosen family and friends. One action to take is right in front of you—the people you care about, the perfect place to start making a difference. Be aware of how you view them and how you could see them even more fully through your four Lenses:

Spiritual, Emotional, Mental, and Action. Celebrate your connectedness and the differences that make them unique teachers for you. Communicate with intention, meaning and love.

Now that the book is in your hands, I have some steps of my own to take: After all the sacrifice she's made these last years, I'm giving my wife the actual "quality time" and emotional intelligence that I talk about in this book and have done too little of lately. I'm really looking forward to some walky-walky with her. She deserves it. I think I'll buy her a car, too. NOT a Prius (inside joke)!

My kids are growing up fast, with their own interests and directions in life. I see how we are changing the way our family engages with each other—the camping trips, vacations, holidays, and all of the ways we've gotten together as a family over the years. Some of those ways are going to be different as we all change. I'm committing to seeing my kids as they are, appreciating how they're growing, and taking action to do more planning around them, as well as other chosen family and friends.

> **My friend, Rob Soper, has been one of my** staunchest supporters of writing this book. Whenever I saw him, Rob would ask, "How's *our* book coming?" He's not too far off because when we're together, we always get into deep conversations about our businesses, the world and life... at which point he would grab me by the shirt sleeves and shake me (and he's a very big guy) to say, "Hey, that should be in the book!" In fact, some things are, which I think will surprise him! I appreciate

Rob. We need those people in our lives with whom we can share something earth-shattering or lousy or great.

Business associates and community organizations. You build your community by being a community. Another action you can take is to practice reaching out to your broader community, nourishing relationships and connections you already have, and making new ones happen through your Lenses and human gifts. Whenever I do that, I find that I really do see different things when I look at them differently: new ways to give, receive, have a good time, and learn!

To help spark your imagination, here are some of the community groups my company, my family, and I continue to serve. Many of them have appeared in the book, for good reason—the impact they have made on us and the services we've offered them.

- Business associates, suppliers, customers and service providers, Tao of Pizza podcast guests, and the Rise 25 company
- Business organizations: Warehousing Education and Research Council, American Frozen Food Institute, International Society for Service Innovation Professionals, International Association of Refrigerated Warehouses, Global Cold Chain Alliance, Council of Supply Chain Management Professionals
- Community organizations: Friends of the Napa River project, Ag4Youth Ranchers, Cycle for Sight road bike events, The Father's House church and ministry, Levi's Gran Fondo world cycling event, Napa Christian School, Wounded Warrior Project®, Graffiti USA Museum

MY COMMUNITY TO YOURS

Henry David Thoreau wrote in his book *Walden*: "Most men live lives of quiet desperation." I think many people are just going through the motions of living, conforming to societal expectations while suppressing their authentic selves and passion. My passion is to live the exact opposite of that AND to be a spark that inspires others to live more freely, peacefully, and prosperously.

So, I say to you, without any BS: **I am a resource for you.** Connect with my website: https://taoofpizza.com/, through my company, Specialized Storage Solutions, or via email. Our team is committed to being a resource for the readers of this book. If you have an idea of something you want to create, beautiful! Whatever we can do to help you start a company, write a book, or start a movement, we will provide resources to connect you with opportunities in our ecosystem.

We're going to be here to help!

This is your kingdom, your dash, your Whole Person path... your life.

"If we are related, we will meet."

And I hope that, through these pages, we have met—and will meet again.

WRAPPIN' IT UP: A POEM BY MARK HIDDLESON
(Annotated)

If I wrote a book ...

It would be a map to the moon for stars.
> *Map is a great metaphor if you know where you are, where you want to go, AND are willing to do what it takes to get there. Make your moonshot "map" matter to mentors, ancestors and future generations.*
> *"We're all stars" is not just a bougie t-shirt or coffee mug.*

When they all get the point,

They'll aim for Venus or Mars.
> *Spiritual lens generates possibilities of impossibilities.*
> *Emotional, Mental, and Action lenses create the space for what's possible.*
> *Mentors have done what's necessary, what's possible, and often what seemed impossible.*

And all of a sudden realize

We won't get there in electric cars.
> *Insanity is doing the same thing over again and expecting different results. Henry Ford would have designed a faster horse. Let's transform transportation again.*
> *It's walky-walky. Train your body, and your mind will follow.*

But by discovering who and what is truly Ours.
> *We're beings that harness solar radiation to generate a human within an ecosystem of billions of other beings.*
> *Plotinus, Plato, Lao Tsu, Jesus, Copernicus, Galileo, Newton, Einstein not Feinstein.*
> *Being is becoming. Practice what you preach.*

If you want to save gas,

Fart in jars.
> *Emotional connection to the past blinds us to real opportunities.*
> *Spiritual teachers or leaders should piss you off a little.*
> *Love is action.*

Einstein proved we're all stars;

Why the fuck would we go to Mars?
> *Socrates would have reasoned that knowing everything is "one thing"; we would choose accordingly.*
> *Science has proven his point that we're woven from the same fabric as everything else in the universe.*
> *We don't act or think like it at all.*

I get it; it's simple.

Your neighbor's a pimple.
> *Love your neighbor as you love yourself. Simple, yet not easy.*
> *Life is short; eternity is real; people matter most.*
> *Sometimes people suck. Love them anyway, and hang out with those who "get it."*

As stars with souls, we're free to love, wander, and roam.
> *Free from worry, guilt, shame and unrealistic social pressure.*
> *We can be the difference that makes a difference.*
> *In our health, family and community.*

I finally realized,

The most important map is the well-worn path home.
> *Home is a peaceful sanctuary.*
> *Home is a state of feeling connected at the deepest energetic level to everything that is.*
> *Life is a process of journeys out and returning home.*
> *Do the math and make your path your own.*

That is what this book is all about

And I hope when you read it,

From a hilltop, you'll shout,

"Read this book and GIVE US A SHOUT OUT!"

ACKNOWLEDGMENTS

This book has been a team effort since its inception, so I want to acknowledge some of the people who have contributed to this project.

Bettyanne Green: Thank you for your expertise as a writing partner and manuscript advisor. You've taken my writing and, without losing my voice, made it a much better read. And thank you for creating the space for this project to unfold. Your challenging yet supportive questions have strengthened the message. Thank you for being a collaborator, confidant, and friend.

Michelle Prince and the team at Performance Publishing: I love the way you have supported this project. I extend my deepest gratitude to those whose exceptional support made this journey possible. Your clear and consistent communication, Judy Pryschlak's surgical editing, and the talented design group brought this project to life in ways I could only imagine. Thank you, Nicole Marsolek and Nancy Acevedo, for your consistent guidance and unwavering encouragement throughout the publishing and marketing process. Your dedication and professionalism have been invaluable, and I am truly grateful for the opportunity to collaborate with such an outstanding team.

To my close family and friends—Chris Johnson, Robert Soper, Danny Peterson, Stacey Peterson, Mike Cardoso, Ty Fyuller, Rob Zwolinski, Jeff Sproull, Nancy Fateen, Tony Caetano, Micah Perez, Jon McCown, Brandon Peterson, and Nik Liebe—your unwavering support, encouragement, and sometimes even well-placed skepticism (Danny, I'm looking at you) kept me motivated. Whether through a simple check-in or deep conversations over a glass (or more) of wine, your presence in my life means the world to me.

I am also indebted to the mentors, influencers, and thought leaders who have shaped my journey—Sal Fateen, Chris Murphy, Michael Mikitka, Joe Ferris, Michael Thomas, Danny Medina, Steve Waller, Matt Burke, David Smith, Vicki Dello Joio, Shawn Phillips, and John Allen Mollenhauer. Your wisdom, guidance, and insights played a crucial role in shaping the content and direction of this book.

A heartfelt thank you to Andrew Green and Lenore Hirsch for reviewing early drafts and providing invaluable feedback that helped refine the final version. I also want to recognize *The Tao of Pizza* podcast guests, whose stories, research, testimonials, and case studies enriched these pages.

To my professional network and collaborators—including colleagues, partners, and organizations such as The Warehouse Education and Research Council, Rise25, International Society of Service Innovation Professionals, Friends of the Napa River, Ag4Youth, and the Business Alliance of Local Living Economies—your support, resources and shared expertise made this project stronger.

To my readers: Thank you for engaging with this book's message. Your curiosity and willingness to explore new ideas are what make this journey meaningful.

To all of the JFK'ers: You know who you are! We practiced creating space, holding containers, non-judgment, and new ways of being, and we shared our gifts in inspiring ways that still amaze me. Every time I connect with a JFKU alum, there's a certain undeniable energy and presence. Thank you for the contribution you made to my life and this work.

My children—Drake, Kody, and Sarena—have played an integral role in this book's creation. Drake and Kody provided early feedback, shaping the chapters long before they took their final form, while Sarena brought the book to life with her beautiful graphics. I could not be prouder of the thoughtful, talented, and kindhearted adults they have become.

Finally, to my wife, Casey. Your love, patience, and belief in me have been my greatest source of strength. Through every late night, every moment of doubt, and every step of this journey, you stood by my side. This book, like so much in my life, would not have been possible without you.

With deep gratitude,
mh

CHAPTER NOTES AND CITATIONS

WHY YOU WANT TO READ THIS BOOK

I wrote the Tao of Pizza because the Tao of Physics was too hard. I once was at the Scottish Rite temple (San Francisco, CA) for an event honoring Stanislav Grof, one of the principal developers of transpersonal psychology. I met Dean Ornish and Michael Pollan and shared a few close moments with Grof himself. But Fritjof Capra stole the networking show. Reaching into his pocket, he handed me a postcard for his online course, a personal touch that outshone everything. I've never read *The Tao of Physics*, but I have read *Turning Point* and *The Hidden Connections* and studied Capra's work in grad school. He remains my networking hero.

Fritjof Capra. *The Tao of Physics*. Shambhala Publications, Boulder, CO, updated edition 2010.
https://www.shambhala.com/the-tao-of-physics-1462.html

"The more you lose yourself in something bigger than yourself, the more energy you will have."
Norman Vincent Peale. *The Power of Positive Thinking*. Prentice Hall, Englewood Cliffs, NJ, 1952.

"The purpose of life is to discover your gifts and the meaning of life is to share them."
At 18, I resented my father (for all of the right reasons), and wounds festered for almost two decades. But I extended the invitation to reconcile so my kids

could get to know their grandparents. We rebuilt our relationship through family occasions, sports games, dance, and musical performances—shared laughs, stories, and much love. Years turned into cherished decades. At his passing, 25 years later, I grieved not just a father but a close friend.

"Within [the tetrahedron] lies the energy that holds all life together." To dive deeper into Buckminster Fuller's study of geometry to help our understanding of systems, here is a source from the Buckminster Fuller Institute: https://www.bfi.org/about-fuller/big-ideas/systems/

WHY ME?

I really sat up and paid attention when Bob Milano, head baseball coach at the University of California-Berkeley, got up to speak. He is still a distinguished figure in collegiate baseball, renowned as the head coach of the University of California, Berkeley's Golden Bears baseball team from 1978 to 1999. He was the winningest coach in the program's history and was inducted into the American Baseball Coaches Association Hall of Fame in 2010. What really impresses me is that Bob Milano is known for playing a pivotal role in developing future MBA talent as a trusted mentor.

Lifestyle of "sex, drugs, and rock and roll" refers to a 1977 song by Ian Dury, who popularized the phrase, which became a catchy rallying cry for the rebellious spirit of the late 1970s—emblematic of the counterculture's excesses and freedoms. My close friends and I added our own flair to the concept in the 80s and 90s. These are still some of my top priorities, but I now enjoy them in a way that doesn't hurt others.
Malcolm Dome, "The Story Behind The Song: Sex & Drugs & Rock & Roll by Ian Dury. *Classic Rock*, December 31, 2016.
https://www.loudersound.com/features/story-behind-the-song-sex-drugs-rock-roll-by-ian-dury

Edward Lorenz's Butterfly Effect. Edward Lorenz posits that in a complex, nonlinear system such as the weather, small variations in initial conditions can produce vastly divergent outcomes—akin to how a butterfly flapping

its wings in one part of the world might influence a tornado elsewhere. The concept has come to represent how an individual's thoughts, emotions, or intentions can have a far-reaching impact on the larger web of interconnected energy.
Edward N. Lorenz. "Deterministic Nonperiodic Flow." *Journal of the Atmospheric Sciences*, vol. 20, no. 2, 1963, pp. 130-141.
https://journals.sagepub.com/doi/10.1177/0309133308091948

INNERCHAPTER: WE BE TREES! (Nature as our guide)

Trees symbolize interconnectedness and community. The concept of the Woodwide Web originated in a series of scientific papers led by the forest ecologist Suzanne Simard.
Suzanne Simard. *Finding the Mother Tree: Discovering the Wisdom of the Forest.* Vintage Books, New York, 2022.
Finding the Mother Tree
https://www.theguardian.com/commentisfree/article/2024/jul/09/wood-wide-web-theory-charmed-us-bitter-fight-scientists

CHAPTER ONE: Spiritual Lens — Possibility

"Let's take just one example: the act of breathing." Source: Deepak Chopra. *Perfect Weight: The Complete Mind/Body Program for Achieving and Maintaining Your Ideal Weight.* Crown Publishing, 1994.

"Humankind has not woven the web of life." I first encountered this quote on a bottle of Picayune Cabernet in a Calistoga wine-tasting shop. Less than a year later, we found ourselves vacationing in Argentina with the winemaker, Claire Durocq Weinkauf, as our amazing transformational cross-cultural tour guide. Claire operates a captivating wine-tasting and gift shop, where her remarkable hospitality and winemaking expertise create an experience that delights all six senses.
https://www.linkedin.com/in/claire-weinkauf-2250775/
https://picayunecellars.com/

Albert Furtwangler. *Answering Chief Seattle*. University of Washington Press, Seattle, 1997.
https://uwapress.uw.edu/book/9780295976334/answering-chief-seattle/

"Knowing others is wisdom; knowing yourself is Enlightenment." Lao Tzu. *Tao Te Ching*. Translated by Stephen Mitchell, Harper & Row, New York, 1988, Chapter 33.

My colleague, John Allen Mollenhauer (JAM), is a leading Performance Lifestyle® Coach and co-founder of Regenus Center, which he cofounded with his partner and wife, Mariahna Suzan.
https://regenuscenter.com/provider/john-allen-mollenhauer/

"People who have faith in life are like swimmers." Brother David Steindl-Rast is an Austrian-born Benedictine monk renowned for his teachings on gratitude and interfaith dialogue. His ideas are referenced throughout the transformative *Book of Joy*, conversations between the Dalai Lama and Archbishop Desmond.
David Steindl-Rast. *Gratefulness, the Heart of Prayer: An Approach to Life in Fullness*. Paulist Press, New York,1984.
https://www.paulistpress.com/Products/2628-1/gratefulness-the-heart-of-prayer.aspx?srsltid=AfmBOoqDKQ1SrGIrKW8wLvnak-_tc3CGXBHcWYkflY59JK47LrlGpLVa

"Don't judge each day by the harvest you reap but by the seeds you plant." Attributed to Robert Louis Stevenson, the 19th-century Scottish author best known for works like *Treasure Island* and *Strange Case of Dr Jekyll and Mr Hyde*. Despite the lack of a verifiable source, the sentiment remains popular in inspirational literature and quotation collections—so we're going with the flow.

"Real religion transforms anxiety into laughter." This is one of many quotes by Alan Watts in the book because he's my guy. Alan Watts (1915–1973) was a British philosopher, writer, and speaker known for popularizing Eastern philosophy for Western audiences. Watts was ordained as an Episcopal priest in 1945, but he left formal ministry in 1950, finding organized religion

too rigid for his broader exploration of spirituality. Instead, he became a captivating lecturer and writer who blended humor, wisdom, and accessible language to convey complex spiritual ideas. His works explore spirituality, mindfulness and the interconnectedness of life, with insights from Christian theology, Zen Buddhism, Taoism, and Hinduism.
Alan W. Watts. *There is Never Anything but the Present: And Other Inspiring Words of Wisdom*. Pantheon Press, New York, latest edition 2020.
For more wisdom from Alan Watts: https://alanwatts.org/

One of my favorite shows is *South Park*. For laughs and discomfort, visit: https://southpark.cc.com/

We start with the idea that your worldview creates the realm of what's possible. The concept of the "materialist paradigm" is described fully in *The Turning Point*. Fritjof Capra describes the materialist paradigm as a worldview rooted in Cartesian dualism and Newtonian mechanics, emphasizing reductionism, linear causality, and the physical as primary reality. This paradigm underpins Western science, technology, and economics, often neglecting interconnectedness, systemic thinking, and the spiritual dimensions of life.
Fritjof Capra, *The Turning Point: Science, Society, and the Rising Culture*, Bantam Books, New York,1984.

It is narrated that in the 1870s...
Man and Superman: A Comedy and a Philosophy, a four-act play by George Bernard Shaw. Archibald Constable & Co. Ltd., London, 1903.

"The perfect man uses his mind as a mirror; it grasps nothing, refuses nothing, receives but does not keep." I was introduced to Chuang Tzu by Vicki Dello Joio, and later interviewed Solala Towler on my podcast.
The Inner Chapters: The Classic Taoist Text, the works of Chuang Tzu translated by Solala Towler. Watkins Publishing, London, 2010.

Napa, California, a world-class traveler's destination, lies in the flood-prone valley of the Napa River. While in grad school, I studied the Napa River project and joined the Friends of Napa River to volunteer, creating and

distributing flyers, etc. My family has supported the effort financially, and I'm still actively involved.
About the Napa River/Creek Flood Protection Project: https://www.countyofnapa.org/1083/Napa-RiverCreek-Flood-Protection-Project
About Friends of the Napa River: http://www.fonr.org/

"The individual is the aperture through which the whole energy of the universe is aware of itself." This is a terrific answer to the question, Who am I? Watts, *There is Never Anything* (2021).

"Perhaps we'll never know how far the path can go…" George Leonard, author and Aikido master, explores the principles and mindset required to achieve mastery in any endeavor, stressing the importance of consistent practice, patience, and a long-term perspective. In this work, he draws on personal experiences and insights from psychology to illustrate how individuals can progress from novice to expert over time.
George Leonard, *Mastery: The keys to success and long-term fulfillment*. Plume (an imprint of Penguin Group), New York, 1992.

CHAPTER TWO: Emotional lens — Passion

Emotions are something we physically feel. Authenticity Associates Coaching & Counseling is a professional practice dedicated to helping individuals and organizations achieve genuine self-awareness, emotional well-being, and personal growth. Through tailored coaching and counseling services, they guide clients to align their values, develop healthier relationships, and cultivate more fulfilling lives. https://www.authenticityassociates.com/emotions-are-energy/#:~:text=What%20we%20think%20of%20as%20emotion%20is%20the,word%20emotion%2C%20%E2%80%98emotere%E2%80%99%2C%20literally%20means%20energy%20in%20motion.

"Until you make the unconscious conscious, it will direct your life and you will call it fate." For more exploration of these ideas attributed to Carl Jung:

C.G. Jung. *Aion: Researches into the Phenomenology of the Self*. In *Collected Works of C.G. Jung*, Vol. 9 (Part 2). Princeton University Press, Princeton, NJ, 1959.
https://press.princeton.edu/books/hardcover/9780691097596/collected-works-of-c-g-jung-volume-9-part-2?srsltid=AfmBOorIfa6_dn-E7dSUovRdaRYz4mLPhr8Cxl4pv_7gQkmyGr8Q8X30

Poet Linda Ellis invites: *"Your life is made of two dates and a dash [on your tombstone]."*
https://lindaellis.life/

Figure 3: Zig Ziglar's Wheel of Life. Note that the seven sections on the wheel are titled slightly differently on Ziglar's website. The Hiddle-Haddle version differs slightly from what we found on Zig Ziglar's current website.
https://www.ziglar.com/articles/the-wheel-of-life/

CHAPTER THREE: Mental Lens — Pronunciation

The Spiritual Lens and Emotional Lens are containers for the Mental Lens. Reference to "determinist terms" prompts some curiosity about determinism. If so, here is my take and a source to dive into: Determinism is a philosophical view that all events, including human actions, are determined entirely by preceding causes, leaving no room for genuine freedom of choice. This would imply that, given the same exact initial conditions, there is only one possible outcome for any chain of events. No freedom, no choice? Sounds great. Sign me up!
Carl Hoefer. "Causal Determinism." *The Stanford Encyclopedia of Philosophy* (Fall 2022 Edition), edited by Edward N. Zalta.
plato.stanford.edu/entries/determinism-causal

"Watch your thoughts, they become words..." This version is most often attributed to Ralph Waldo Emerson, yet it does not appear in his major collections. The quote has also been attributed to people like Frank Outlaw and Lao Tzu, but its exact origin remains unclear. Either way, Ralph Waldo Emerson referred to this concept and so many others as a

profoundly influential American philosopher whose writings on individualism, self-reliance, and transcendentalism have inspired generations of writers, thinkers, and social reformers.
Ralph Waldo Emerson. *Essays: First Series*. James Munroe and Company, Boston, 1841.

"It is something to be able to paint a particular picture..."
Henry David Thoreau. *Walden*. Edited by J. Lyndon Shanley, Princeton University Press, Princeton, NJ, 1971, "Conclusion" chapter; originally published by Ticknor and Fields in 1854.
https://press.princeton.edu/books/hardcover/9780691061948/the-writings-of-henry-david-thoreau?srsltid=AfmBOoo1CGM-5PYswziR1A7Q b0MExKRckjXlhgOoFfzkDxYmd0G9L77

Bonnie Artman Fox shared Tasha Eurich's study findings.
Tasha Eurich. *Insight: Why We're Not as Self-Aware as We Think, and How Seeing Ourselves Clearly Helps Us Succeed at Work and in Life*. Crown Business, New York, 2017.
https://www.tashaeurich.com/
For more information on Bonnie Artman Fox, Executive Coach as well as Accredited Boss Whisperer® Coach:
https://bonnieartmanfox.com/
https://www.bosswhispering.com/
https://www.specialracks.com/post/how-to-correct-abrasive-leadership-and-improve-conflict-management-styles-with-bonnie-artman-fox

Tell a More Optimistic yet Realistic Story... This is something I learned from John Allen Mollenhauer (JAM).
Mollenhauer: https://regenuscenter.com/provider/john-allen-mollenhauer/

One powerful shift I learned from Wendy Palmer was to say *yes, and...* instead of *yeah, but...* I worked for many years with Wendy Palmer, and she was a great influence on me. She was the founder of Leadership Embodiment, a process that uses principles from the non-violent Japanese martial art of Aikido and mindfulness. Her work was about offering simple tools and practices to increase leadership capacity and respond to stress and pressure

with greater confidence and integrity. She held a seventh-degree black belt in Aikido. Although she passed away in 2022, her daughter and business partner, Tiphani Palmer, continues to run the organization.
https://leadershipembodiment.com/

"Finding your voice is Effectiveness, and helping others find their voice is Greatness."
Stephen Covey. *The 8th Habit: From Effectiveness to Greatness (The Covey Habits Series)*. Free Press, New York, 2005.

"Words are, in my not-so-humble opinion, our most inexhaustible source of magic."
Source: Quote by Albus Dumbledore in *Harry Potter and the Deathly Hallows: Part 2*
https://www.imdb.com/title/tt1201607/
J.K. Rowling, *Harry Potter and the Deathly Hallows*, Bloomsbury Publishing (UK); Scholastic (US); Raincoast Books (Canada), 2007.

John Mackey, the founder of Whole Foods, used the complaints they received. Source: The Awakening Leadership Program: https://awakening-leadership.org

"Be 'hearty in your approbation and lavish in your praise'..."
Dale Carnegie, *How to Win Friends and Influence People: Updated For the Next Generation of Leaders*. Simon & Schuster, New York, 2022.

The reason? Holding the tetrahedron in your hands... Active learning, which involves the student's direct participation and experiential engagement, leads to better memory retention and understanding. This enhancement is attributed to increased "synaptic plasticity," the ability of synapses (the connections between neurons) to strengthen or weaken over time in response to increases or decreases in activity—fundamental to learning, memory, and overall brain function.
https://www.sciencedirect.com/science/article/pii/S0149763424002069

CHAPTER FOUR: Action Lens — Practice

One day, while enjoying lunch on the Napa River... Ron Zwolinski is a Pharmaceutical Operations Executive and a good friend and professional colleague. Our workouts, rides, and lunch conversations provided initial support and continued encouragement to complete this project.

"Our task is to free ourselves from this prison." Albert Einstein's essay captures his reflections on compassion, interconnectedness, and human responsibility toward nature and all living beings.
Albert Einstein. *The World as I See It*. Collection of essays, Philosophical Library, New York, 1949.

"The gift of practice excels all gifts..." This is a modern adaptation of Dhammada (verse) 354, where "practice" replaces "Dhamma", emphasizing the lived application of the Buddha's teaching rather than the teaching itself. Here is the canonical version, which is part of the Pali Canon and translated into English by Acharya Buddharakkhita:
"The gift of Dhamma excels all other gifts;
the taste of Dhamma excels all other tastes;
the delight in Dhamma excels all other delights.
He who has destroyed craving overcomes all sorrow."
Eknath Easwaran, author/translator, *The Dhammapada*. Nilgiri Press, Petaluma, CA, revised edition 2007.
Known for its poetic rendition of the original Pali text:
Juan Mascaro, translator. *The Dhammapada: The Path of Perfection*. Penguin Books, Harmondsworth, UK, 1973.

"It is often the space inside the vessel or the doorway which seems of no substance..."
Towler. *The Inner Chapters* (2010)

In his book, *12 Rules for Life*, Canadian clinical psychologist Jordan Peterson shares... This is one of the top ten books that I've never read. I've watched some of his presentations on YouTube. The Human Highlight

Show, "Treat yourself like someone you are responsible for helping," which includes a short clip explaining this rule.
Jordan B. Peterson. *12 Rules for Life: An Antidote to Chaos* (book #1 in the Rules for Life Series). Penguin Books, New York, 2019.
https://www.youtube.com/watch?v=RY0tReBbfMA

"Are you paralyzed by fear? That's a good sign. Fear is good."
Steven Pressfield. *The War of Art: Break Through the Blocks and Win Your Inner Creative Battles*. Black Irish Entertainment LLC, Los Angeles, 2002.
https://blackirishbooks.com/product/the-war-of-art/

My long-time friend, Chris Murphy, is not afraid to grab the mic at any event.
Chris Murphy is a Renaissance Man, CEO and President of a third-generation business, Sierra Pacific Warehouse Group, publisher of the *ModestoView*, musician, cruise enthusiast, and supporter and active community builder. He appears in this book a lot because he is that kind of guy and has had an immense influence on me. Sierra Pacific Warehouse Group: www.spwg.com
https://www.linkedin.com/in/spwgchris/
Socials: @modestochris
Modesto View: www.modestoview.com

In *God and the Evolving Universe: The Next Step in Personal Evolution...*
James Redfield, Michael Murphy & Sylvia Timbers. *God and the Evolving Universe: The Next Step in Personal Evolution*. TarcherPerigree (a division of Penguin Random House), New York, 2003.
https://www.penguinrandomhouse.com/books/288689/god-and-the-evolving-universe-by-james-redfield-michael-murphy-and-sylvia-timbers/

"Whether you face reality head on and make a life change, or deny your responsibility, you've made a choice." Shawn Phillips, the Philosopher of Fit, is a Father, Author, Entrepreneur, ADD Empowered Creator, and Advocate for Awakening.
Shawn Phillips. *Strength for Life: The Fitness Plan for the Rest of Your Life*. Ballantine Books, New York, 2008.
https://www.linkedin.com/in/shawn-phillips-3723b/

https://x.com/Shawn_Phillips
https://www.facebook.com/shawn.b.phillips

"So, what should we do? Anything, something..." From 1992 to 1997, I was a Gold Certified Chrysler sales consultant. I learned this concept as part of the training involved.
https://www.britannica.com/money/Lee-Iacocca

INNERCHAPTER: FDA Approves First Meditation Pill (a parody)

Jamie Wheal is the co-founder of the Flow Genome Project, an organization dedicated to mapping the science of peak performance and flow states. As of this writing, they have not found a singular "gene" responsible for this state.
https://www.flowgenomeproject.com/

CHAPTER FIVE: Economic Lens — Profession

"No one on his deathbed ever said, 'I wish I had spent more time on my business." In 1983, Senator Paul Tsongas received a personal letter from his friend Arnold Zack, a labor arbitrator and mediator, after Tsongas decided not to seek reelection due to a cancer diagnosis. Zack's quote encouraged Tsongas—who had been weighing his health and family against the demands of public office—to focus on what mattered most in life. Tsongas later shared this message widely, helping the line become a popular reminder that time and relationships often outweigh professional ambitions, especially when facing life's finite nature.

Chris Johnson is a teacher, coach, spiritual seeker, and my friend. He and I have discussed this quote and many other deep philosophical questions. We share a passion for all things spiritual. Deep connections don't always require words—true friends understand each other beyond conversation. Quote source:

https://quoteinvestigator.com/2021/03/31/deathbed-wish/#:~:text=No%20one%20on%20their%20deathbed,'
Chris Johnson: @coachjohnson54

The cradle-to-grave or "waste equals food" approach to business represents a paradigm shift in companies' operations. The idea of cradle-to-grave (or cradle-to-cradle) challenges the traditional linear economy by proposing that all materials remain in continuous cycles, rather than the landfill. The aim is to eliminate the very concept of waste by designing products and processes to be biodegradable or repurposed indefinitely without harming the environment.
William A. McDonough and Michael Braungart. *Cradle to Cradle: Remaking the Way We Make Things*. North Pole Press, New York, 2002.

For a long time, I believed podcasts were just a time-suck... but I soon found that guesting on and hosting podcasts was a great way to connect to others, thanks to John Corcoran and Dr. Jeremy Weisz, cofounders of Rise 25. Their company helps B2B businesses get more clients, referral partners, and strategic partners through their podcast service.
Rise 25: www.Rise25.com
John Corcoran:
http://www.linkedin.com/in/corcoran
Dr. Jeremy Weisz:
https://www.linkedin.com/in/drweisz/

Now I host my own podcast, which I call the Tao of Pizza, of course! Available on Apple, iHeart, Spotify, or wherever you get your podcasts. Subscribe!
Blog | Special Racks
https://taoofpizza.com/
https://open.spotify.com/show/5Abczx04zSulWV0nAHf0xg

In the bustling world of warehousing and logistics... Michael Mikitka is Executive Vice President of Warehousing Education and Research Council (WERC), a division of the Material Handling Industry (MHI). Michael and WERC fostered my personal and professional growth very early in my career.

He even got me a seat next to Hall of Fame running back Emmit Smith at a National Convention in Chicago.
WERC: werc.org
Full interview with Mike Mikitka: https://www.specialracks.com/post/the-art-and-science-of-leading-leaders-through-event-production
Warehousing Education and Research Council
American Logistics Aid Network:
https://www.alanaid.org/

INNERCHAPTER: An Ecology of Values (Sow the seeds of peace and prosperity)

"Sow a thought and you reap an action ..."
Emerson, *Essays* (1841).

CHAPTER SIX: Effort Lens — Patience

"The ability to dominate nature is what many believe to be the secret of security..."
Theodore Roszak was an American historian, social critic, and professor, renowned for his influential work, *The Making of a Counter Culture* (1969). He often critiqued the modern pursuit of technological dominance over nature, suggesting that true security and civilization lie in aligning ourselves with ecological processes. He promoted a vision of cultural transformation rooted in ecological harmony and spiritual depth.
Theodore Roszak. *The Making of a Counter Culture: Reflections on the Technocratic Society and Its Youthful Opposition.* Doubleday & Company, Inc., New York, 1969 (A widely-cited later edition was published by the University of California Press in 1995).

Richard Strozzi-Heckler is an amazing person I've been following for years. His books inspired me to pursue graduate study in the area of Mind-Body connection. I mistakenly thought he was an instructor at JFK University.

Apparently, there is another Somatic Psychology and martial arts-based teacher in the California Bay Area named Richard Heckler. Richard Strozzi-Heckler. *In Search of the Warrior Spirit: Teaching Awareness Disciplines to the Green Berets* (Revised). Blue Snake Books, Berkeley, CA, revised 4th edition, 2007.
https://strozziinstitute.com/staff/richard-strozzi-heckler/

Tony Caetano and I met as young professionals, and from the beginning, I admired his thoughtful and authentic approach to business relationships. Over time, and especially through our conversations around the content and creation of this book, our friendship has deepened into something truly meaningful. A combat veteran, Tony has continued to serve others—particularly fellow veterans—with dedication and heart. I am deeply honored by his service and even more moved by his openness in sharing that this book has helped him navigate the effects of PTSD. Knowing it may help others through his experience gives this work greater purpose. I am profoundly grateful for Tony's friendship, wisdom, and unwavering support.

"Success is peace of mind, which is a direct result of self-satisfaction..." To learn more about John Wooden's legacy and philosophy, visit: https://coachwooden.com/

"The worst teacher is one who thinks they have nothing left to learn." "Drake H" is my youngest son. His wisdom extends well beyond his years.

One great example is the company I mentioned earlier, called Rise 25. Weisz and Corcoran https://rise25.com/about/

One day, Jeremy shared a line from a song called "Cruise." Florida Georgia Line created some of the most popular recordings in country music's history by embracing hip-hop and rock influences. In less than a decade, Brian Kelley and Tyler Hubbard amassed 25 gold, platinum, or multi-platinum singles, with two—"Cruise" and "Meant to Be"—reaching diamond sales certification. Very few artists in any genre have accomplished that feat.
https://www.youtube.com/watch?v=fmgmJLE-Mql

"Life and love generate effort, but effort will not generate them."
Watts, *There is Never Anything* (2021).

When I was young, I heard a speech given by a well-known business expert, Skip Ross.
https://skipross.com/

INNERCHAPTER: Be an Agent of Chill

"Everything is energy and that's all there is to it..." This quote is not Albert Einstein's and there are physics people pissed off that it gets passed on like it is! I don't find any source for this quote. The point is that he said the essence of this was in everything he did. So, you can look it up yourself.

#1: Posture. Rule number... "Stand up straight with your shoulders back." Peterson, *12 Rules for Life* (2019).

CHAPTER SEVEN: Tuning Lens — Pertinacity

"If you want to awaken all of humanity, then awaken all of yourself..."
Lao Tzu. *Tao Te Ching*. Translated by Stephen Mitchell, Harper & Row, New York, 1988, Chapter 33. https://www.biblio.com/9780060160012?srsltid=AfmBOoo10tbooZBtCWZ6kZvzpw7H0ydPmdupecCRAguH-HrAhLAllg9L
For more quotes attributed to Lao Tzu: https://www.goodreads.com/author/quotes/2622245.Lao_Tzu?page=6#:~:text=Quotes%20by%20Lao%20Tzu%20(Author%20of%20Tao%20Te%20Ching)

Growth mindset. You have probably heard this term related to business. Carol S. Dweck, Ph.D., *Mindset: The New Psychology of Success*. Random House, 2006.
https://www.vitalsource.com/products/mindset-carol-s-dweck-v9781588365231
Article: https://hbr.org/2016/01/what-having-a-growth-mindset-actually-means

THE TAO OF PIZZA | 321

"A path is made by walking on it." Attributed to Chiang Tzu (also known as Zhuangzi), Chinese philosopher and author, known for his Taoist philosophy Towler, *The Inner Chapters* (2010).

The amazing Greg Bateman, author of *Steps to an Ecology of Mind*, challenges us. On my birthday, riding a rented bicycle through Monterey, CA, I discovered a small bookstore, hunting for something else entirely. But bookstores have a way of deciding for you. Wandering through the shelves, I stumbled upon *Steps to an Ecology of Mind* by Gregory Bateson—a book I hadn't planned to find but somehow felt like it had found me. Bateson's collection of essays explores the intricate patterns of thought, communication, and nature, weaving together anthropology, psychology, and cybernetics into a philosophy of interconnectedness. His idea that "the pattern that connects" is essential to understanding life itself resonated with me as I pedaled home, the ocean breeze carrying the feeling that maybe nothing is ever truly random—not even the books we find when we're looking for something else. Gregory Bateson. *Steps to an Ecology of Mind: Collected Essays in Anthropology, Psychiatry, Evolution, and Epistemology.* Originally published by Chandler Publishing Company, 1972; later reprints include the University of Chicago Press edition (2000).
https://press.uchicago.edu/ucp/books/book/chicago/S/bo3620295.html
More goodies about Greg Bateman: https://www.architectural-review.com/essays/an-ecology-of-mind

"ROMO" is usually related to pandemic loneliness or avoiding the internet. Tony Romo's 2016 press conference: https://youtu.be/nw1GXGIFtVA

"The only way to make sense out of change is to plunge into it, move with it, and join the dance." Watts, *There is Never Anything* (2021).

Diving deeper into the surfing world-as-life.
Srinivas Rao, *Unmistakable: Why Only Is Better Than Best.* Portfolio Books, imprint of Penguin Random House, New York, 2016.
Srini's guest interview on the *Tao of Pizza* Podcast: https://sites.libsyn.com/419696/website/knowledge-management-best-practices-with-srinivas-rao-1

CHAPTER EIGHT: Circular Cyclical Lens — Process

Think about growing up believing that 2+2=4, then finding out that 2+2 ALSO equals 6 (xx)! In Anti-Math, unconventional rules are applied to standard arithmetic operations, leading to non-traditional results such as 2 + 2 = 6.. These exercises highlight how manipulating foundational mathematical principles can produce unexpected outcomes. Here's a visual demonstration:
https://youtu.be/1Orbvbep2hI?si=Jn2n59VxojIJoRBj

"The Edge... There is no honest way to explain it."
Hunter S. Thompson. *Hell's Angels: A Strange and Terrible Saga*. Random House, 1967 (reprinted many times by various publishers since).

One such figure is Saint Francis of Assisi.
Augustine Thompson, O.P. *Francis of Assisi: A New Biography,* Cornell University Press, Ithaca, New York, 2012.

"Tell me, what do you plan to do with your one wild and precious life?"
From the poem "The Summer Day".
Mary Oliver. *House of Light*. Beacon Press, Boston, 1992.

In 1950, Stanford pre-med student Michael Murphy... Michael Murphy co-founded the Esalen Institute in 1962, creating a pioneering center for human potential, alternative spirituality, and mind-body exploration. His vision brought together Eastern and Western philosophies, psychology, and personal development, influencing movements in transpersonal psychology, holistic health, and consciousness studies. Through Esalen, Murphy helped shape a cultural shift toward self-exploration, meditation, and integral practices that continue to inspire personal and societal transformation. Murphy, Redfield & Timbers. *God and the Evolving Universe* (2003)
https://www.esalen.org/about

Michael Murphy has enjoyed a front row seat at the Human Potential Movement longer than I've been here on this planet. The Integral Life podcast did a three-part interview with him; you can watch the full series here:

https://integrallife.com/the-human-potential-movement-then-and-now/

Ron Mikus was a close friend and business associate. Some people walk into your life and quietly rearrange the furniture of your mind, making space for ideas you never dared to believe in. Ron was one of those rare souls—a burning flame in the night, a steady hand on my shoulder when doubt crept in. With gentle but unwavering conviction, Ron saw potential in me before I could see it myself. His words, "Grow a pair of balls and… " were like flint striking steel, igniting the fire that became my business. And when belief wasn't enough, he backed it with action, offering not just wisdom but the financial support that turned dreams into reality.

Though Ron is no longer here in body, his spirit lives on in every risk I take, every lesson I pass forward, and every success I celebrate. His guidance wasn't just a gift—it was a legacy; one I carry forward with gratitude and determination.

Sal Fateen has been one of the most influential figures in my life, both personally and professionally. I originally sought to connect with him because of his impressive business network, but what I didn't expect was how much he would come to mean to me as a mentor and friend. Over the years, he's become like family—someone I turn to for advice, wisdom, and support. Sal's vast experience in the industry, coupled with his genuine kindness and generosity, has had a profound impact on me. From our first meeting at a jazz festival to becoming close friends who share life's milestones, Sal has been a constant presence in my journey. His guidance has shaped not only my career but also my understanding of what true leadership and friendship look like.
https://www.seizmicinc.com/about/
https://www.linkedin.com/in/sal-fateen-5636302b

"We seldom realize that our most private thoughts…"
Watts, *There is Never Anything* (2021).

"'Wu wei', directly translated, means not overdoing, over-extending, pushing the river, or forcing something to happen. Solala Towler teaches and practices Taoist meditation and qigong. He has authored, co-authored, or translated approximately twelve books on Taoism and related subjects, including notably: *Tales from the Tao, Tao Paths to Love, Practicing the Tao Te Ching*, and *Cha Dao: The Way of Tea, Tea as a Way of Life.*

Solala Towler. *Tales from the Tao: Inspirational Teachings from the Taoist Masters.* Watkins Publishing; Illustrated Edition, April 2017.

You can watch the interview with Solala on my *Tao of Pizza* podcast: https://www.specialracks.com/post/principles-of-taoism-with-solala-towler

INNERCHAPTER: The Practice of Freedom

The gap between spirituality and science began to diminish with the growing popularity of the publication. In 1969, Harvard physician Dr. Herbert Benson conducted pioneering research on Transcendental Meditation (TM), demonstrating its physiological benefits, including reduced metabolism, heart rate, and blood pressure. This study laid the groundwork for his concept of the "relaxation response," a state counteracting stress-induced fight-or-flight reactions, advancing the scientific understanding of meditation's health benefits.

Herbert Benson, MD. *The Relaxation Response*, William Morrow & Company, New York, 1975, reissued since by various publishers.

Here's a video where Dr. Benson describes the relaxation response: https://youtu.be/nBCsFuoFRp8

CHAPTER NINE: Community Lens — Procreation

"Life is short. Eternity is real, and relationships matter most." Pastor Dave and The Father's House have impacted my spiritual journey fantastically! I have never been a fan of organized religion or formal pastoral leadership. Dave and the team at The Father's House deliver on the promise of BEing a place to connect and experience God's presence.
https://tfh.org/

"The next Buddha will manifest not in one person but in a collective, a sangha."
https://plumvillage.org/articles/true-sangha

The International Society of Service Innovation Professionals (ISSIP) is a diverse global community. Michele Carroll exemplifies the power of *collective intelligence*—the synergy that emerges when individuals come together, share knowledge, and solve problems in ways no single person could achieve alone. As the founder and president of Carrollco Marketing Services and the Executive Director of ISSIP, Michele has been a driving force in business innovation, helping companies gain market traction, secure funding, and grow their influence. Her belief in people-centered service innovation underscores the importance of human connection in a technology-driven world. I'm grateful for her contributions, her insights, and the example she sets as a leader who brings people together to create something greater than the sum of its parts.
https://issip.org/
Check out my interview with Michelle Carroll on the Tao of Pizza podcast: https://www.specialracks.com/post/the-power-of-human-centered-innovation
More information on Michelle Carroll, founder and president of Carrollco Marketing Services and Executive Director of ISSIP: https://carrollcomarketing.com/staff-member/michele-carroll/

"You ARE your network." Mick Mankowski was one of my dad's best friends, and having him as a guest on my podcast brought back wonderful memories of my father. Mick has continued to keep me on his exclusive "friends only" email list, a gesture that means a lot. I was honored to host one of my earliest business heroes, Mick Mankowski, on *The Tao of Pizza* podcast. Watch our full conversation for insights, stories, and lessons from a true master of networking.
https://www.specialracks.com/post/surviving-the-floods-of-change-in-logistics-and-apparel-with-mick-mankowski

"History has shown that any man who would significantly change the world must have showmanship..." *Cat's Cradle* is Kurt Vonnegut's critique of the potential loss of human autonomy in a technologically dominated world. In this book, I've drawn on these ideas to create a fictional character, Professor Vaughn, who embodies the perspectives of three college professors I had—each of whom shared similar values. They believed that government is fundamentally the legitimate use of force, that technology can stifle creativity and autonomy, and that utopian visions often spiral into dystopian realities. Their insights continue to shape my thinking about power, progress, and the unintended consequences of idealism.

Kurt Vonnegut, *Cat's Cradle*. Viking reissue edition, 2011; first published Holt, Rinehart and Winston, 1963, Chapter 58.

The company began to get "corporatized."
Whizty Kim, "What happened to Airbnb?" Vox.com, November 8, 2023. https://www.vox.com/money/23941827/airbnb-complaints-guests-cleaning-fee-new-york-regulation

Have you seen the movie *American Graffiti*? The Graffiti USA Museum was founded in Modesto, CA, to share, educate and inspire visitors with exhibits that showcase postwar popular culture, including classic cars, the rise of rock and roll, radio and the pastimes of the 1950s, 60s and 70s that captivated America—all that inspired Modesto native George Lucas to create his landmark film *American Graffiti*, paving the way for his future creations like *Star Wars* and *Indiana Jones!*

American Graffiti, directed by George Lucas, Universal Pictures, 1973: https://www.imdb.com/title/tt0069704/

Graffiti USA Museum: https://www.graffitiusamuseum.com/

On July 17, 2023, members of 17 car clubs and other interested citizens filled the city council chambers to voice their support.
Rich Ibarra. *SacramentoKnow Newsletter*, Capradio.com, July 17, 2023. https://www.capradio.org/articles/2023/07/17/modesto-ends-33-year-ban-on-cruising/

Chris Murphy: "When we bring our cultures together, our community shines…"
Murphy. *SacramentoKnow (2023)*.

INNERCHAPTER: The Natural Evolution of Social, Economic, and Structural Networks (a history)

Our civilizations change over time. But what about our psychologies? The Spiral Dynamics Model was first developed by Clare Graves, Don Beck, and Christopher Cowan to illustrate a series of developmental stages by different value systems and cognitive frameworks. Ken Wilber popularized Spiral Dynamics, using it as a tool to map out the different levels of human consciousness and development, incorporating it into his broader Integral Theory. https://spiraldynamics.org/resources/books/

Ken Wilber's book was one of the first I read about the evolution of psychology. I couldn't find his book on the shelf, so I asked the clerk about getting a copy. She promptly found one in the back, but when she returned, she gave me a puzzled look and said, "Are you sure this is the book you're looking for?" Don't judge a book by its cover! Ken Wilber's *Sex, Ecology, Spirituality: The Spirit of Evolution* explores the evolution of consciousness and reality through an integral lens. Blending science, philosophy, and spirituality, Wilber proposes a comprehensive framework for understanding the interconnected development of individuals, societies, and the cosmos, emphasizing holistic approaches to ecology, culture, and transcendence. I studied his work extensively in grad school at JFK University.
Ken Wilber. *Sex, Ecology, Spirituality: The Spirit of Evolution*. Boston: Shambhala Publications, 1995.

THE END...And an Invitation to Begin

Vicki Dello Joio, one of my favorite teachers, is an expert on what she has coined "spiritual fitness." She is a Qigong Master Teacher, Speaker/Storytelling Mentor, and owner of Way of Joy: A Spiritual Fitness Program and Your Power Presence, and author of The Way of Joy. I had the privilege of studying with Vicki during graduate school, where she deeply influenced my journey through multiple weekend retreats and later as a businessperson in her coaching programs.

Vicki Dello Joio. *The Way of Joy: An evolutionary process to awaken inspiration, focus intention, and manifest fulfillment.* Wyatt-MacKenzie Publishing, Oregon, 2009.
https://www.vickidellojoio.com/
https://www.linkedin.com/in/vickidellojoio/ https://www.facebook.com/vickidj

My friend, Rob Soper, has been one of my staunchest supporters and a constant source of encouragement. Every time we meet, our conversations naturally turn to business, the world, and life's bigger questions. Rob has a way of challenging ideas, pushing for deeper thinking, and making sure nothing important goes unsaid. We all need people like Rob—those who push us, challenge us, and make life's journey richer. I'm grateful to have him in mine.
Water Connections
Love it or Shove It
https://www.linkedin.com/in/rob-soper-8187a479/

Business organizations:
Warehousing Education and Research Council
https://werc.org/
American Frozen Food Institute
https://affi.org/affi-con/?gad_source=1&gclid=Cj0KCQiAx9q6BhCDARIsACwUxu5X9Rfrnh231olGEijrMVGcD8g7sKvIWRNV9yyJS-xKyIvhTDAzk-saAgsOEALw_wcB
International Society for Service Innovation Professionals
https://issip.org/
International Association of Refrigerated Warehouses
https://www.refrigeratedfrozenfood.com/keywords/4728-international-association-of-refrigerated-warehouses
Global Cold Chain Alliance
https://www.gcca.org/
Council of Supply Chain Management Professionals
https://cscmp.org/

Community organizations:
Friends of the Napa River project
http://www.fonr.org/
Ag4Youth Ranchers
https://ag4youthnapa.org/
Cycle for Sight road bike events
https://battistrada.com/en/cycling-calendar/edition/cycle-for-sight-wine-valley-2024/27629/
The Father's House church and ministry
https://www.tfh.org/visit?gad_source=1&gclid=Cj0KCQiAx9q6BhCDARIsACwUxu6khHOC0B4GjDXgZU4iqmB5yjcn8qQDqSXgmnF95mBRWphfL-J8RYmsaAqzpEALw_wcB
Levi's Gran Fondo world cycling event
rb.gy/nm3sm8
Napa Christian School
https://www.napachristian.com/
Wounded Warrior Project®
https://support.woundedwarriorproject.org/Default.aspx?tsid=11585&ovr_acv_id=20344&campaignSource=ONLINE&source=BS24032AAABREAA&gad_source=1&gclid=Cj0KCQiAx9q6BhCDARIsACwUxu5V1UTPjemtAPxLVp0kaJCMaR7zLb-I89TbQTtvzQd5n25rrLIevHIaAuw9EALw_wcB&gclsrc=aw.ds
Graffiti USA Museum
https://www.graffitiusamuseum.com/

"If we are related, we shall meet." Attributed to Ralph Waldo Emerson. In his essay "Friendship," Emerson discusses the natural attraction between kindred spirits, suggesting that those who are meant to connect will inevitably do so. He writes, "Friends also follow the laws of divine necessity; they gravitate to each other, and cannot otherwise."
Emerson, *Essays* (1841).

HOW TO CONTACT MARK HIDDLESON

Mark Hiddleson is a seasoned entrepreneur with decades of experience in the warehousing and logistics industry. A leader in several professional organizations, he is passionate about optimizing supply chains, enhancing operations, and fostering professional development through a holistic approach. With expertise in negotiation, warehouse safety, facility layout and design, and public speaking, he has dedicated his career to driving innovation and efficiency in his field.

Guided by a belief that nature offers the ultimate blueprint for balance and sustainability, he applies a holistic perspective to business and leadership. By observing natural systems, he draws insights on adaptability, efficiency, and resilience—principles that shape his approach to logistics, entrepreneurship, and personal growth.

Beyond his professional achievements, Mark is a devoted husband and father, an engaged community member, and the host of *The Tao of Pizza podcast*, where he explores business, leadership, and personal growth. As an author, he shares his insights on industry trends, entrepreneurship, and the power of connection, inspiring others to navigate challenges and seize opportunities in both business and life.

http://www.linkedin.com/in/mark-hiddleson-1b8584b/

https://www.taoofpizza.com/

www.ingramcontent.com/pod-product-compliance
Lightning Source LLC
Chambersburg PA
CBHW070606170426
43200CB00012B/2600